CORINNE CRASBERCU

MY RAG DOLL

Photography by Frédéric Lucano
Stylists: Sonia Lucano and Vania Leroy-Thuillier
Text by Dominique Montembault

D&C
David and Charles

CONTENTS

When I was little, I used to spend hours dressing my dolls and playing with them, and before long, as soon as I learned how to knit, embroider and sew, I began to make them. For this, I owe thanks to my mother and father (master of the old Singer machine!) as well as my grandmother.

Inspired by the world of Sarah Kay and Beatrix Potter, I used to unearth old sheets and scraps of fabric, lace and ribbons from the bottoms of trunks in the attic to make my dolls, especially their clothes... dresses, skirts, little tops and all kinds of little accessories.

That was how my passion for sewing, clothing and fashion began and how it became my career!

Let me help you discover a world where the magic of childhood is still alive. A world that is well within your reach!

MAKING THE DOLL

All the dolls are made from the same pattern (see doll template). The body and head are the same, only the facial expressions and the hair change. Carefully follow the instructions below, then turn to pages 9-14 to create the faces. Enlarge the faces using a photocopier or take inspiration from the different models to make your own unique doll.

Materials

Doll template
Old sheet dyed with tea, 40 x 60cm (16 x 21in)
Polyester wadding (batting)
Pins

Sewing and embroidery needles
Tacking thread
Sewing thread, beige

1 Enlarge the pattern pieces for the doll by 140% using a photocopier, and cut out. Cut out the pattern for the arms and legs twice in mirror image.

2 Fold the fabric in half and, ensuring the arrows are sitting on the grainline, pin all the pieces onto the fabric, with the centre of each leg placed along the fold to obtain a single piece. Only the back and front of the head are pinned to a single thickness of fabric. Cut out all these pieces with a 1cm (½in) seam allowance. Insert pins to mark the notches.

3 Start by reducing the back of the head. Gather the top of the head between the notches, so that the back and the front of the head are the same size.

4 Using a sewing machine, join the two half-fronts of the body along the centre and attach the front of the head to the top, at neck level. Do the same with the two half-backs and the back of the head, but leaving a large opening in the centre of the back seam. Position these two pieces on top of one another, right sides together, and sew along the sides, shoulders and all around the head, leaving an opening to insert the arms. Turn the body of the doll right side out.

5 Place the two pieces of fabric that form the arms on top of one another, right sides together, and sew all the way around, leaving one side open. Turn the arms out and fill with wadding (batting).

6 Join the top of the feet to the bottom of the legs, ensuring that the right and left feet are in the correct position, and close up the darts. Fold the fabric in half, right sides together, and sew along the length. Attach the bottom of the foot to the top of the foot using tacking thread, and then sew by machine. Turn the legs right side out and fill with wadding (batting), ensuring they are filled equally. Fit the legs and arms into the openings on the body, and attach them with a line of machine stitching along the inside edge.

7 Fill the head of the doll with wadding (batting), then the body, and close the back seam with small, invisible stitches.

For the Ballerina doll and the Little Fairy doll, enlarge the pattern pieces by 120%.

BLONDE DOLL

Doll in pink (page 40) • Bedtime doll (page 70)

Materials

Cotton yarn, vanilla
DMC Mouliné Stranded Cotton 819 (powder pink),
3031 (chocolate brown), 3771 (peach pink),
3833 (petal pink) and Ecru

Tissue paper
Adhesive tape

1 Make 11 skeins each of 15 strands of vanilla yarn, 50cm (20in) long, cutting their ends. Arrange nine skeins flat, side by side, across a width of 18cm (7in), and tape them in the middle (on top and underneath). Place a strip of tissue paper under the adhesive tape and machine stitch down the middle before removing the paper and the adhesive. Fold in half along the line, adjust the hair on the head, 1cm (½in) behind the seam, and sew using small stitches. Fold the hair down well at the back, apart from a little lock that you can let fall freely on each side. Secure the hair on the back of the head using backstitch, level with the ears.

2 Lay the two remaining skeins flat, side by side, across a width of 6cm (2½in), and tape them in the middle (on top and underneath), to form a parting. Place a strip of tissue paper under this parting, sew a line of stitching on top by machine and remove the paper. Position this hair on the doll's forehead, allowing it to overlap the hair at the back by 1cm (½in). Stitch to the head using little stitches along the parting. Attach the two locks of hair either side of the head using a few stitches level with the ears and tie them together at the back with a strand of cotton thread.

3 Embroider the eyes using stem stitch with two strands of brown stranded cotton (floss). Start at the centre and embroider in a circle to the desired size. To give them sparkle, make a little French knot from ecru stranded cotton (floss). The mouth is made from a curve embroidered using stem stitch, with two strands of petal pink stranded cotton (floss). The nose, just above, is made from a bullion knot, with two strands of powder pink stranded cotton. For the cheeks, embroider two circles using satin stitch, with two strands of peach pink stranded cotton (floss), spacing out the stitches.

BRUNETTE DOLL

Floral doll (page 26) • Fairy doll, large (page 102)

Materials

Wool, chocolate brown
Blue cotton ribbon, 2 x 15cm (6in)
DMC Mouliné Stranded Cotton Ecru, 413 (stormy grey),
3771 (peach pink) and 4200 (red/orange colour variation)

Tissue paper
Adhesive tape

1 Make seven skeins of 12 strands of chocolate brown wool, 60cm (23½in) long, and cut their ends. Make another consisting of eight strands, 10cm (4in) long.

2 Place the large skeins of wool flat, side by side, and tape them in the middle (on top and underneath), to form a parting. Place a strip of tissue paper under this line, machine stitch line on top then remove the paper and adhesive.

3 Do the same for the little skein that will act as the fringe. Fold this in half and sew by hand using little stitches at the top of the doll's forehead. Place the scalp of hair on top, centering the parting and allowing the hair to come over the fringe to disguise where it starts. Attach to the head using little stitches along the parting, then plait the hair and tie with a piece of ribbon. Sew a few stitches in chocolate brown wool on either side of the head, level with the cheekbones, to hold the braids in place.

4 Embroider the eyes using stem stitch with two strands of stormy grey stranded cotton (floss). Start at the centre and work in a circle to the desired size. To give them sparkle, make a little French knot in each eye in ecru stranded cotton (floss). The mouth is made from a little circle of satin stitch with two strands of red/orange stranded cotton (floss). Create a nose with a bullion knot in two strands of ecru stranded cotton (floss). For the cheeks, use satin stitch and two strands of peach pink stranded cotton (floss), spacing out the stitches.

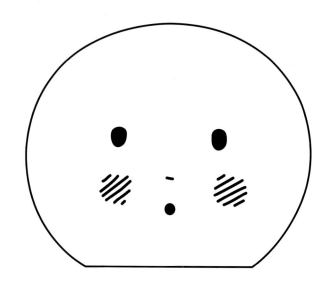

RED-HEAD DOLL

Doll in dungarees (page 20) • Doll in red (page 32) • Doll with stars (page 56) • Doll in blue (page 78)

Materials

Wool, rust brown
DMC Mouliné Stranded Cotton, ecru,
413 (stormy grey), 4130 (rust colour variation)
and 4200 (red/orange colour variation)

Tissue paper
Adhesive tape

1 Make seven skeins of 12 strands of wool in rust brown, 60cm (23½in) long, and cut their ends. Make another consisting of eight strands, 10cm (4in) long.

2 Place the large skeins of wool flat, side by side, and tape them in the middle (on top and underneath), to form a parting. Place a strip of tissue paper under this line, machine stitch a straight line before removing the paper and adhesive.

3 Repeat this process with the little skein that will act as the fringe. Fold this in half and sew by hand using little stitches at the top of the doll's forehead. Place the scalp of hair on top, centring the parting and allowing the hair to come over the fringe to conceal the join. Attach to the head by sewing little stitches along the parting, then tying the hair on either side. Fold these bunches in half and attach them with a strand of rust brown wool, making them puff out at the front.

4 Embroider the eyes using stem stitch with two strands of stormy grey stranded cotton (floss). Start at the centre and embroider in a circle to the desired size. To give them sparkle, make a little French knot in each eye in ecru stranded cotton (floss). For the mouth, embroider a little circle using satin stitch and two strands of red/orange stranded cotton (floss). Create the nose with a bullion knot and two strands of ecru stranded cotton (floss). For the cheeks, stitch five running stitches in a circle, 1½cm (⅛in) in diameter and one stitch in the middle with two strands of rust stranded cotton (floss).

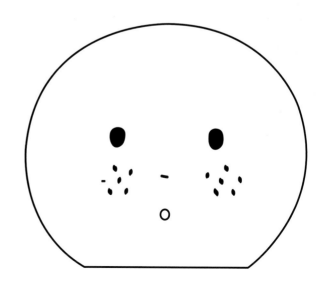

AUBURN, DARK BLONDE AND GINGER DOLL

Bride doll (page 48) • Doll with strawberries (page 64) • Doll in raincoat (page 94)

Materials

Very fine Mohair wool, brown (auburn doll), very light yellow (dark blonde doll) or orange (ginger doll)
DMC Mouliné Stranded Cotton 3705 (coral pink), 819 (powder pink), 310 (black), in ecru, 894 (candy pink) and 930 (blue)

Knitting needles, size 7mm, 6.5mm (US10.5), 5.5mm (US9)
Crochet hook, 3mm (D3)
Pink ink
Fine marker pen

1 Make a cap on which to hang the hair. Using 7mm needles and mohair, cast on 47 sts, change to 6.5mm needles. Beginning with a knit row work 3cm (1 ¼in) in stocking (stockinette) stitch ending on a knit row. Change to 5.5mm needles and decrease on purl rows only as follows:

First dec row: Slip 1, (p3, p2tog) to last st, k1 - 38 sts.

Second dec row: Slip 1, (p2, p2tog) to last st k1 - 27sts.

Third dec row: *P1, p2tog, rep from * to end - 18 sts.

Fourth dec row: P2tog to end - 9 sts.

2 Pass a thread through remaining sts and pull tight then fold in half and sew the seam. For a small head circumference (for the little dolls), cast on 38 or 42sts, according to the thickness of the wool, and proceed in the same way purling any extra sts left over at the end of the decrease rows.

3 Attach the cap to the head of the doll with a few little stitches.

4 Cut some strands of wool, 60cm (23½in) long. Fold a strand of wool in half. Push the crochet hook into a stitch of the cap and bring the tip out on the reverse of the cap.

Catch the loop of the strand of wool and pull to make it come out on the right side of the cap. Thread the ends of the strand of wool through the loop and pull to attach to the cap.

5 Start by attaching the strands around the circumference of the head and continue on the central part of the cap to create a parting. Attach the strands of wool every two or three rows evenly spaced, and cut off any strands that are too long, as well as the strands at the front to make a fringe or short hair.

6 Dab the cheeks in a circle with the pink ink. For the auburn doll, embroider the mouth with two strands of coral pink stranded cotton, the eyes using stem stitch with two strands of black stranded cotton (floss) and finish by making the nose with a French knot and two strands of powder pink stranded cotton (floss).

7 For the dark blonde and ginger dolls, embroider the mouth with two strands of candy pink stranded cotton (floss), the eyes using stem stitch with two strands of blue stranded cotton (floss) and finish by making the nose with a French knot with two strands of ecru stranded cotton (floss).

The dark blonde doll and the ginger doll are made in the same way. For the ginger doll, add a few freckles on the cheeks with a fine marker pen.

RAVEN-HAIRED DOLL

Fairy doll, small (page 109)

Materials

Wool, black
DMC Mouliné Stranded Cotton 310 (black),
ecru, 894 (candy pink)

Tissue paper
Adhesive tape

1 Make the scalp for the black-haired doll as for the blonde doll (see page 11).

2 Embroider the eyes with two strands of black stranded cotton (floss), the nose with a French knot with two strands of bright pink stranded cotton (floss) and the mouth with two strands of ivory stranded cotton (floss) following the design.

Auburn, dark blonde and ginger-haired dolls

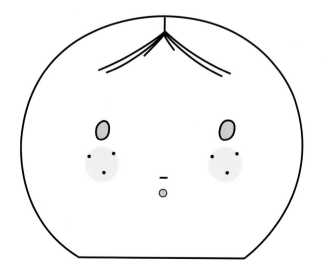

Raven-haired doll

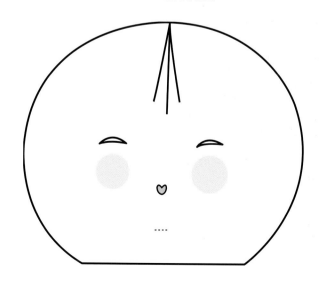

NEEDLECORD

Ballerina doll (page 86)

Materials

(see pattern page 116)
Brown needlecord, 15 x 40cm (6 x 16in)
DMC Mouliné Stranded Cotton 3031 (brown),
3326 (soft pink), 819 (powder pink)

Iron-on velvet, scrap
Pink ink

1 Turn under the fabric along the long edges and press lightly with an iron. Fold this rectangle in half along the length, right sides together, and sew the ends.

2 Turn right side out and machine stitch a line in the middle to form a parting. Run a gathering thread along the front of this line for 4cm (1½in), and gather the fabric to achieve a width of 1½cm (⅝in)

3 Hand stitch the needlecord strip to the front of the head, positioning it at the centre of the forehead, and sewing a few stitches at the back, at the base of the neck.

4 Pass a gathering thread along each side, level with the ears, gather the fabric and hold it tight with a piece of embroidery yarn. Sew the ends together and hang them at the back of the neck.

5 Dab the cheeks in a circle using pink ink. Embroider the mouth with two strands of soft pink stranded cotton (floss) and the nose in a French knot with two strands of powder pink stranded cotton (floss). Cut out the eyes from the velvet and attach them using an iron.

BLOOMERS

1 Enlarge the pattern for the half-bloomer (page 117) by 140%, and cut out two copies. Fold some cotton voile in half, in the direction of the grain, and pin the two pattern pieces to it, with the long side along the fold. Cut the fabric, allowing 1cm (½in) for the seam allowance and the fabric to be turned under at the top, and 2cm (¾in) for the hem at the bottom.

2 Fold each half-bloomer in half, right sides facing, and sew a line along the legs to close them up. Pin the two half-bloomers together, right sides together, and sew the inside leg seam. Oversew these seams.

3 Fold the waistband over to the inside of the bloomers, turn under a small amount of fabric and stitch, ensuring that you leave an opening. Thread a piece of flat elastic through this gap to adjust the waist to 23cm (9in) and sew the two ends firmly together.

4 Turn under the bottom of the legs to the inside, level with the fold. Turn under a small amount of fabric and stitch it all the way around, leaving a little opening level with the seam to thread the elastic through. Sew a second, parallel line of stitching, 8mm (⅜in) apart, all the way around. Thread 10cm (4in) of thin elastic through the resulting channel and tie the ends together. Sew a piece of scalloped broderie anglaise to the bottom of each leg, then turn the bloomers right side out.

5 Tie two decorative bows in pink ribbon and stitch one to the outside of each leg, level with the elastic. Sew a little heart button to the centre front, level with the waistband, with two strands of pink stranded cotton (floss).

VEST

1 Enlarge the pattern for the half-back and front (page 116) by 140%, making two copies, and cut out these two pieces. Fold some cotton voile in half, in the direction of the grain, and pin the two pattern pieces to it, with the centre back and centre front along the fold. Cut the fabric allowing 1cm (½in) for the seam allowance and the fabric to be turned under at the top and 2cm (¾in) for the hem at the bottom. Insert a pin at the armhole notch.

2 Pin the sides up to the armholes, sew a line of stitching, then finish off with a hem either side of these armholes. Oversew the seams.

3 Turn under the top of the back by 1cm (½in) to the reverse, turn under a small amount again and stitch to make a channel. Thread a piece of flat elastic through the channel to adjust the width to 9cm (3½in) and attach the elastic on either side using a few hand stitches.

4 Pass a gathering thread around the top of the front and gather until it is 9cm (3½in) wide. Tack a piece of scalloped broderie anglaise to these gathers, as well as some tape, to the right side of the fabric. Oversew the three thicknesses of fabric together. Turn the tape over to the reverse, tuck in the sides and attach them to the front of the vest using a few hand stitches.

5 Cut two straps 10cm (4in) long from some fine lace and sew the ends to the top of the back and front, on the reverse using little stitches. For the front, attach them to the broderie anglaise having turned under the ends. Sew a heart button centrally at the front, beneath the embroidery lace, with some stranded cotton (floss) in pink. Finish the vest by sewing a hem at the bottom, and topstitch it on the right side with a running stitch using pink stranded cotton (floss).

✄ DOLL PATTERN

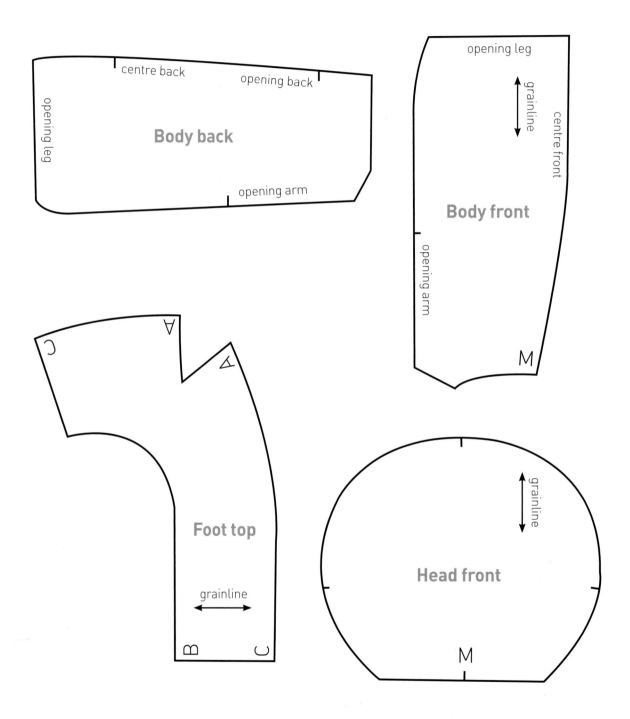

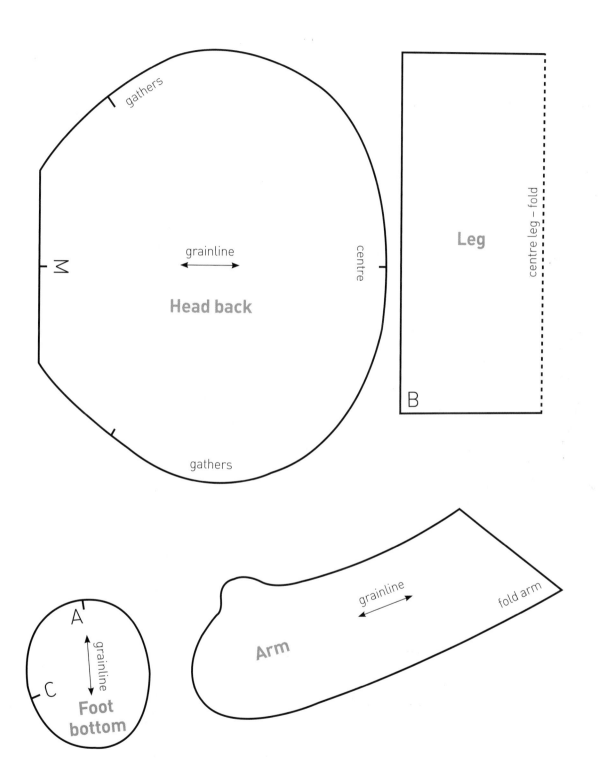

gathers

M

grainline

centre

Head back

gathers

Leg

centre leg – fold

B

A

grainline

C

Foot bottom

grainline

Arm

fold arm

DOLL IN DUNGAREES

 DOLL IN DUNGAREES

Materials

Blouse (pattern page 124)

Beige floral cotton, one fat quarter
Red ric rac, 50cm (20in)
Red tape, 17cm (6½in)
White button with 4 holes, 8mm (⅜in) diameter
DMC Mouliné Stranded Cotton 304 (red)

Boots (pattern pages 118-119)

Canvas, 40 x 20cm (16 x 8in)
Red felt, 15 x 10cm (6 x 4in)
White cord, 20cm (8in)

Dungarees (pattern page 120)

Blue and white striped fabric, one fat quarter
Beige cord, 6cm (2½in)
Jeans buttons x 2
Red felt, scrap

Neckerchief

Red checked cotton, 26 x 26cm (10½in)
White button with 4 holes, 8mm (⅜in) diameter
DMC Mouliné Stranded Cotton 304 (red)

Equipment

Pins
Sewing needle and embroidery needle
Sewing thread in beige, rust brown and red

BLOUSE

1 Enlarge the different pattern pieces for the blouse by 140%, and cut the pieces out: two half-sleeves, a half-back and half-front.

2 Fold the fabric in half in the direction of the grain and pin on the pattern pieces. The half-sleeves and half-front are positioned on the fold. Cut the fabric, allowing for a 1cm (½in) seam allowance and 2cm (¾in) for the hems.

3 Join the two half-backs and the front along the shoulder seams, then oversew. Make a 1½cm (⅝in) box pleat at the centre of the neckline and sew it on the reverse for a length of 3cm (1¼in). Insert the sleeves into the armholes, sew them and close up the sleeves and the sides. Oversew all the seams.

4 Cut the tape in half along the whole length and oversew one of the pieces by machine. Attach the ric rac on top of the oversewn tape and stitch along the neckline, on the right side of the fabric, then turn the tape over.

5 Hem around the ends of the sleeves and the bottom of the blouse, as well as along each of the overlaps at the back.

6 Place some ric rac on each sleeve, 5mm (¼in) from the end. Stitch a button at the top of the opening at the back using two strands of red stranded cotton. Sew a red button loop opposite.

BOOTS

1 Enlarge the different pattern pieces by 140% and cut them out: a sole, upper and leg piece. Fold the canvas in half and pin on the leg piece and upper of the boot. Fold the felt in half and pin on the sole.

2 Cut out the pieces, adding a 1cm (½in) seam allowance all around.

3 Close up the front darts in the uppers, then pin the upper to the leg pieces, and stitch. Topstitch 2mm (¹⁄₁₆in) from the seam.

4 Fold the fabric under at the top of the leg pieces and stitch before closing the back seam of the boots. Join to the soles by lining up the notches at the back and front. Trim the soles to 3mm (⅛in) from the seam.

5 Tie a bow with the cord and sew it to the centre front. Make the second boot in the same way.

DUNGAREES

1 Enlarge the pattern pieces for the dungarees by 140% and cut the pieces out: a front half-leg, back half-leg, strap, trouser pocket, bib and breast pocket. Fold the striped fabric in half in the direction of the grain and pin on the pattern pieces. Only the bib and the little pocket are pinned to a single thickness of fabric. Cut the fabric allowing for a 1cm (½in) seam allowance and 1½cm (⅝in) for the hems.

2 Sew a hem 1cm (½in) wide all the way around the bib and topstitch the top and sides with two lines of stitching 8mm (⅜in) apart.

3 Fold up and tack a hem around the pockets and sew a hem 1cm (½in) wide at the openings, topstitched with two lines of stitching, 8mm (⅜in) apart. Tack the pockets to the front half-legs of the trousers and to the bib, then topstitch. Hem around the armholes at the back and join the two half-backs by the seam at the centre and stitch. Sew a hem 1cm (½in) wide at the top of the back and topstitch two lines of stitching 8mm (⅜in) apart.

4 Pin the front half-legs level with the centre seam and stitch, oversewing the top of the front. Position the bottom of the bib on the top of the front, and topstitch it all with two lines of stitching, 8mm (⅜in) apart. Place the back and the front on top of each other, right sides together, pin and stitch the leg seams and the inside leg seam to close up the trousers, oversewing the seams. Sew a hem at the bottom of each leg. Turn the dungarees right side out. Turn the fabric at the bottom of the legs up 4cm (1½in) to form a turn-up.

5 Sew hems all the way around the braces, and attach one end to the back of the dungarees. Fold the other end up 4cm (1½in), wrong sides together, and stitch 1cm (½in) from the fold to form a channel. Thread a little piece of cord inside, and tie a knot that you can hide in the channel. Attach two buttons to the top of the bib, on either side. Cut out a little red heart from felt and sew in the centre of the breast pocket using little running stitches and beige thread.

NECKERCHIEF

1 Cut the 26cm (10½in) square of fabric diagonally in half to make a neckerchief. Hem all around the edges of the fabric. Stitch a white button to one of the points on the reverse of the fabric with two strands of stranded cotton (floss) in red. Sew a button loop on the opposite point, also on the reverse of the fabric.

FLORAL DOLL

 FLORAL DOLL

Materials

Dress (pattern page 122)

Floral ecru fabric, one fat quarter
Plum and red ric rac, 60cm (23½in)
Ecru tape, 17cm (6½in)
Pink cotton ribbon, 5cm (6in), 1cm wide
Thin elastic, 18cm (7in)
Press studs x 2
Floral button, small

Shoes (pattern page 118)

Red felt, 15 x 35cm (6 x 14in)
Mother-of-pearl buttons with 4 holes,
8mm (⅜in) diameter x 2
Red hook and loop fastening

Pinafore (pattern page 123)

Pink floral fabric, one fat quarter
Mother-of-pearl heart buttons x 2
Striped poplin, 11 x 17cm (4½ x 6½in)
Floral fabric, 4 x 4cm (1½ x 1½in)
DMC Mouliné Stranded Cotton 3806 (pink)

Bag (pattern page 121)

Floral cotton, 16 x 32cm (6¼ x 12½in)
Wooden curtain rings x 2
Red ric rac, 30cm (12in)
Floral button with 2 holes, 1½cm (⅝in) diameter
DMC Mouliné Stranded Cotton 3806 (pink)

Equipment

Pins
Sewing needle and embroidery needle
Tacking thread
Sewing thread in beige, red and pink
Pinking shears

 FLORAL DOLL

DRESS

1 Enlarge the pattern pieces by 140% and cut them out: a half-front and half-back for the bodice, half-front and half-back for the skirt, and sleeve.

2 Fold the fabric in half and pin on the patterns. The half-fronts of the bodice and skirt are positioned on the fold. Cut out the fabric allowing for a 1cm (½in) seam allowance and 1½cm (⅝in) for the hems. Mark the notches with pins.

3 Join the front and the two half-backs of the bodice along the shoulders and the side seams.

4 Gather the top of the front of the skirt to make it the same width as the bottom of the bodice. Do the same for the two half-backs of the skirt. Pin the bodice and the skirt together ensuring that the gathers are evenly arranged, then stitch. Close up the sides of the skirt with a seam and oversew.

5 Topstitch the bottom of the sleeves, then run a gathering thread around the top, from notch A to notch B. Gather, close up the side seams and oversew.

6 Turn the sleeves right side out, join them to the bodice by lining up the notches, then stitch and oversew. Turn the sleeves to the reverse, turn the fabric up by 2½cm (1in), and stitch around the edge of the fabric, leaving a little opening to thread the elastic through. Sew a second, parallel line of stitching, 5mm (¼in) away, all around. Thread each channel with 9cm (3½in) of thin elastic and tie the ends together.

7 Cut the tape in half along its length and oversew one of the pieces. Tack some ric rac and the oversewn tape around the neckline, on the right side of the fabric. Stitch these three thicknesses together then turn the tape over. Stitch ric rac ribbon on the right side of the dress, across the gathers at the back and front.

8 Hem along the overlap of the two half-backs and around the bottom of the dress. Sew two press studs on the back of the bodice to close it up. Tie a bow with the pink ribbon and sew it to the ric rac. Stitch a flower button just above, with some pink thread.

SHOES

1 Enlarge the three pattern pieces by 140% and cut them out. Use pinking shears for the top of the upper. Pin the pattern pieces on to the felt, then cut out leaving an 8mm (⅜in) seam allowance, except for the strap and the opening, which are cut to the edge.

2 Topstitch the opening, then close the upper of the shoe with a seam. Open it out, tack on the sole, lining up the centre of the sole with the centre of the upper, then stitch. Trim the felt to 3mm (⅛in) from the seam and turn the shoe out.

3 Topstitch round the strap, and sew it to the inside of the shoe, 2½cm (1in) from the back seam. Sew on half of the hook and loop fastening to the end of the strap on the inside. Attach a mother-of-pearl button to the strap, above the fastening with red sewing thread. Sew the other half of the hook and loop fastening on to the shoe, positioning it 2½cm (1in) from the seam.

4 Make the second shoe in the same way, reversing the position of the strap and the hook and loop fastening.

PINAFORE

1 Enlarge the pattern pieces by 140% and cut them out. Pin the bottom of the pinafore and the front waistband to a single thickness of floral fabric and the patterns for the bib, strap and back waistband to a double thickness. Pin the pattern for the pocket to a double thickness of striped poplin. Cut out all the pieces, allowing for a 1cm (½in) seam allowance and 1½cm (⅝in) for the hems.

2 Fold the straps in half along the length, right sides together, stitch along two sides and turn out.

3 Place the two pieces for the bib right sides together and stitch the sides. Slip the two straps between these two pieces of fabric and sew across the top of the bib. Turn the bib right side out.

4 Hem the bottom and sides of the large rectangle. Gather up the unhemmed side and adjust it to the length of the front waistband, ensuring the gathers are even. Place the bib to the reverse and tack it to the centre of the gathers. Turn under a little fabric along one long side of the front waistband and tack the waistband with the wrong sides together. Topstitch catching in the bottom of the bib in the line of stitching. Fold the waistband in half, turn under a little fabric on the opposite side and topstitch the front of the pinafore.

5 Hem around the two back waistbands, make a pleat in one of their ends and slip them into one of the openings of the front waistband. Turn under the fabric at each end of the front waistband and close using little stitches, catching the back waistband in the seam at the same time. Sew the end of a strap to each waistband, 6cm (2½in) from the bib.

6 Sew a hem along the opening of each pocket, and turn the fabric under, tacking all around. Arrange the pockets on the pinafore and topstitch the turnbacks.

7 Turn under and tack all around a little piece of floral fabric, position it on the pinafore, across a pocket, and sew it on with large stitches using two strands of pink stranded cotton (floss). To finish, sew small white heart buttons at the top of the bib, under each strap, using some pink sewing thread.

BAG

1 Enlarge the pattern by 140% and cut it out. Fold the fabric in half and pin on the pattern, with the bottom of the bag along the fold. Cut out the fabric allowing for a 1cm (½in) seam allowance, and insert some pins to mark the start of the openings. Sew two strips of ric rac along the length of the fabric, on the right side.

2 Fold the fabric in half, right sides together, and stitch the sides as far as the notches. Hem either side of the openings as far as the top of the bag. Turn under 1cm (½in) of fabric at the top of the back and front of the bag and pass the fabric around the rings. Pin then sew all along just under the ring with large running stitches using three strands of stranded cotton (floss) in pink. Sew a flower button on to the ric rac using the stranded cotton (floss) in pink.

DOLL IN
RED

DOLL IN RED

Materials

Blouse (pattern page 124)

Beige, floral cotton, one fat quarter
Red ric rac, 50cm (19¾in)
Red tape, 17cm (6¾in)
White button with 4 holes, 8mm (⅜in) diameter
DMC Mouliné Stranded Cotton 304 (red)

Shoes (pattern page 118)

Red felt, 15 x 35cm (6 x 14in)
White mother-of-pearl buttons with 4
holes, 1cm (½in) diameter x 2
Red hook and loop fastening

Skirt (pattern page 125)

Red checked cotton, one fat quarter
Flat elastic, 10cm (4in), 1cm (½in) wide
Red ric rac, 60cm (23½in)
Wooden button with 4 holes, (1cm½in) diameter

Cherries

DMC Mouliné Stranded Cotton 304 (red)
and 700 (green), two skeins each
Green satin ribbon, 50cm (20in), 5mm (¼in) wide

Cape (pattern page 126)

Dark red, boiled wool fabric, 40 x 60cm (16 x 21in)
Light red trim, 140cm (55in)
Light red wool

Hair clips with cherries

Small hair clips x 2
Green cotton ribbon, 50cm (20in), 1cm (½in) wide
Red enamel buttons, 1½cm (⅝in) diameter x 2
DMC Mouliné Stranded Cotton 304 (red) and 700 (green)

Hair clips in red

Small hair clips x 2
Red cotton ribbon, 40cm (16in), 5mm (¼in) wide
Red felt, scrap

Equipment

Sewing needle
Tacking thread
Red and green sewing thread
Pinking shears
Adhesive

BLOUSE

1 Enlarge the pattern pieces for the blouse by 140%, and cut out two half-sleeves, a half-back and a half-front.

2 Fold the fabric in half in the direction of the grain and pin on the pattern pieces. Position the half-sleeves and half-front on the fold. Cut the fabric allowing for a 1cm (½in) seam allowance and 2cm (¾in) for the hems.

3 Join the two half-backs and the front along the shoulder seams and oversew. Make a box pleat 1½cm (⅝in) at the centre of the neckline and sew it on the reverse for a length of 3cm (1¼in). Insert the sleeves into the armholes, sew, then close up the sleeves and the sides. Oversew all the seams.

4 Cut the tape in half along its length and oversew one of the pieces by machine. Tack along the neckline, on the right side of the fabric, having placed the ric rac on top of the oversewn tape, then turn the tape over.

5 Hem the sleeves and the bottom of the blouse, as well as each overlap at the back.

6 Place the ric rac around each sleeve, 5mm (¼in) from the bottom. Sew a button at the top of the opening at the back using two strands of red stranded cotton (floss) and sew a red button loop opposite.

CHERRIES

1 Divide each small skein of stranded cotton (floss) in half, and make four pom poms of 2cm (¾in) in diameter.

2 Cut the ribbon in half and tie a knot at each end of the two pieces. Sew a pompom onto each knot and tie the ribbons, making even loops.

SKIRT

1 Enlarge the pattern pieces for the skirt by 140%: a half-back, half-front, waistband and two half-braces.

2 Fold the fabric in half in the direction of the grain and pin on the pattern pieces. The half-front, half-back and half-braces are positioned on the fold. The waistband is pinned to a single thickness of fabric. Cut the fabric allowing for a 1cm (½in) seam allowance and 2cm (¾in) for the hems.

3 Gather the top of the front so that it is the length of the waistband. Join the back and front along the side seams.

4 Fold the back waistband in half, wrong sides together, turn a small amount of fabric under along the length and stitch. Thread a piece of elastic inside so that the back is slightly narrower than the front and attach the elastic either side using a few stitches.

5 Fold the rectangle of fabric for the waistband in half along the length, wrong sides together, and slip inside the top of the front. Turn under a little fabric along each length and stitch all the layers together. Slip the ends of this waistband into the openings of the back waistband and close each side with a line of machine stitching.

6 Fold the braces in half along the length, right sides together, and sew a seam along the length. Turn the braces out, turn a small amount of fabric under at each end and close using little hand stitches. Attach the braces in a 'V' centrally on the back and front waistbands. Sew a little wooden button on to the front braces level with the waistband using red sewing thread.

7 Hem the bottom of the skirt and sew red ric rac all the way around, 2½cm (1in) from the bottom.

SHOES

1 Enlarge the three pattern pieces by 140% and cut them out. Use pinking shears for the top of the upper of the shoe. Pin the pattern pieces on to the felt, then cut the fabric out, leaving a 5mm (⅝in) seam allowance, except for the strap and the opening, which are cut level with the edge.

2 Oversew the opening, then close the upper of the shoe with a seam. Open out the seam, tack on the sole, lining up the centre of the sole with the centre of the upper, then machine stitch. Trim the felt to 3mm (⅛in) from the seam and turn the shoe out.

3 Oversew around the strap and stitch it to the inside of the shoe, 2½cm (1in) away from the back seam. Sew a piece of red hook and loop fastening to the end of the strap on the inside, and attach a mother-of-pearl button on top with some red sewing thread. Sew the other part of the hook and loop fastening to the shoe, positioning it 2½cm (1in) from the seam.

4 Make the second shoe in the same way, reversing the position of the strap and the hook and loop fastening.

CAPE

1 Enlarge the pattern pieces for the cape by 140%: two half-fronts, a half-back and half-hood.

2 Fold the boiled wool fabric in half in the direction of the grain and pin on the pattern pieces. The half-back and half-hood are positioned on the fold. The half-fronts are pinned to a single layer of fabric. There are no hems; the fabric is cut to the edge of the patterns, just add 1cm (½in) extra for the seam allowance.

3 Fold the hood in half and close it up by stitching the back seam. Mark the notches 'A' with pins. Join the back and fronts along the side seams. Tack the hood to the neckline by lining up the notches with the shoulder seams, then stitch by machine. Tack and sew a red trim all around the cape and the hood.

4 Make three small, red pom poms, 3cm (1¼in) in diameter, with the wool, two cords 22cm (8½in) long and a cord 8cm (3¼in) long. Sew a pom pom to one end of each of these cords.

5 Attach the shorter cord to the tip of the hood, and the two others to the top of each side of the front, where the hood joins the cape. To fasten the cape, tie a bow with these cords.

HAIR CLIPS WITH CHERRIES

1 Cut the ribbon in half and tie into two decorative bows. Sew a red button at the centre of each bow with two strands of red stranded cotton (floss).

2 Attach the bows to the hair clips with green stranded cotton (floss).

RED HAIR CLIPS

1 Cut out two rectangles of felt in the size of the hair clips using pinking shears. Cut the ribbon in half and tie a decorative bow with each piece.

2 Sew a bow to the centre of each rectangle then glue the pieces of felt to the hair clips.

DOLL IN PINK

 DOLL IN PINK

Materials

Dress (pattern page 127)

Pink, printed cotton, one fat quarter
Pink tape, 50cm (20in)
Beige, floral trim, 15cm (6in)
Press studs x 2

Bloomers (pattern page 117)

Beige, checked cotton, one fat quarter
Beige ric rac, 50cm (20in)
Pink, satin ribbon, 15cm (6in), 5mm (⅝in) wide
Flat elastic, 23cm (9in), 5mm (⅝in) wide
Thin elastic, 50cm (8in)

Shoes (pattern page 118)

Pink felt, 15 x 35cm (6 x 14in)
Pink, cotton ribbon, 50cm (8in), 1cm (½in) wide
White mother-of-pearl buttons, 1cm (½in) diameter x 2
Pink hook and loop fastening

Mop cap (pattern page 128)

Pea poplin, one fat quarter
Beige, cotton ribbon, 80cm (31½in), 1cm (½in) wide
Flat elastic, 11cm (4¼in), 3mm (⅛in) wide
Beige, embroidered flowers x 2

Equipment

Sewing needle
Tacking thread
Pins
Beige, pink and yellow sewing thread
Pinking shears

DRESS

1 Enlarge the pattern pieces by 140% and cut them out: a half-front and half-back for the bodice, a half-front and half-back for the skirt.

2 Fold the fabric in half in the direction of the grain and pin on the pattern pieces. The half-fronts for the bodice and skirt are positioned on the fold. Cut the fabric allowing for a 1cm (½in) seam allowance and 1½cm (⅝in) for the hems.

3 Starting with the bodice, join the front and two half-backs along the shoulder, oversewing the seams. Stitch a little tape along the neckline and armholes on the right side of the fabric, then fold it over to the reverse and hold in place with a line of topstitching.

4 Gather the top of the front of the skirt to make it the same width as the bottom of the bodice. Do the same for the two half-backs of the skirt. Pin together the bodice and skirt, ensuring that the gathers are evenly arranged, then stitch and oversew the seams. Close up the sides with a line of stitching and oversew. Hem along the overlap of the two half-backs and all around the bottom of the dress. Sew two press studs to the back of the bodice to close it up. Sew a floral trim to the front of the dress, on the seam between the skirt and the yoke.

BLOOMERS

1 Enlarge the pattern for the half-bloomer by 140% and cut out two copies. Fold the cotton voile in half in the direction of the grain, and pin the two pattern pieces to it, with the long length along the fold. Cut the fabric, allowing 1cm (½in) for the seam allowance and the fabric turned under at the top, and 2cm (¾in) for the hem at the bottom.

2 Fold each half-bloomer in half, right sides together, and sew along the legs to close them up. Pin the two half-bloomers together, right sides together, and stitch the inside leg seam. Oversew these seams.

3 Fold over the waistband to the inside of the bloomer. Turn a small amount of fabric under and stitch, ensuring that you leave an opening. Thread a piece of flat elastic through this channel to gather to a size of 23cm (9in) and sew the two ends firmly together.

4 Turn right side out and stitch a piece of ric rac all around, 5cm (2in) from the bottom of each leg. Turn inside out, fold the fabric up again on the inside along the line of stitching, so that the ric rac shows below. Turn a small amount of fabric under and stitch it all around, leaving a little opening in the seam, to thread the elastic through.

5 Sew a second, parallel line of stitching, 8mm (⅜in) apart, all around. Thread 10cm (4in) of thin elastic through each channel, and tie the ends together. Turn the bloomers right side out, tie a decorative bow with the pink ribbon and attach it to the front, level with the waistband.

SHOES

1 Enlarge the three pattern pieces for the shoe by 140% and cut them out. Pin the pattern pieces to the felt then cut the fabric, leaving an 8mm (⅜in) seam allowance, except for the strap and the opening, which are cut level with the edge.

2 Topstitch the opening, then close the upper of the shoe with a seam. Open out the seam, tack on the sole, lining up the centre of the sole with the centre of the upper, then stitch by machine. Trim the felt to 3mm (⅛in) from the seam and turn the shoe out.

3 Topstitch around the strap, and sew this to the inside of the shoe, 2½cm (1in) from the back seam. Sew a little piece of pink hook and loop fastening to the end of the strap, on the inside. Sew the other part of the hook and loop fastening to the shoe, also at 2½cm (1in) from the seam. Tie a decorative bow with 10cm (4in) of pink cotton ribbon, 1cm (½in) wide, and sew it to the centre front of the shoe, just under the top seam, attaching a small, white, mother-of-pearl button on top.

4 Make the second shoe in the same way, reversing the position of the strap and the hook and loop fastening.

MOP CAP

1 Enlarge the pattern pieces by 140% and cut them out: a half-crown, half-headband and two half-brims. Fold the fabric in half and pin on the pieces, all along the fold. Cut out all the pieces, allowing for a 1cm (½in) seam allowance and 1½cm (⅝in) for the hems.

2 Insert two pins on the headband to show where the elastic will go. Fold the fabric in half, right sides together, and stitch the centre back seam. Hem between the pins and leave the sides open. Slip a piece of flat elastic inside the hem and adjust the width to 11cm (4¼in) and sew the elastic to the fabric on either side.

3 Place the two pieces for the brim one on top of the other, right sides together, stitch the outside edge and turn out. Gather the fabric for the headband from one end of the elastic to the other and slip it into the open side of the brim. Turn the fabric under around each piece of the brim, tack to the headband and topstitch the three layers of fabric together. Gather the other side of the headband, pin it to the crown of the mop cap, then stitch and oversew.

4 Sew a beige ribbon, 80cm (31½in) long, on the line of stitching between the brim and the headband using small stitches and attach a little flower either side at the start of the brim.

BRIDE
DOLL

 BRIDE DOLL

Materials

Dress (pattern page 129)

Ivory poplin, 75 x 24cm (29½ x 9½in)
Ivory lace, 80 x 25cm (31½ x 10in)
Ivory silk, 16 x 20cm (6¼ x 8in)
Lace heart (or other motif)
Ivory lace, 90cm (35½in), 5mm (¼in) wide
Ivory, satin cord, 20cm (8in)
Small mother-of-pearl bead buttons x 4
Flat elastic, 34cm (13½in), 3mm (⅛in) wide

Underskirt

Ivory, fine tulle, 102 x 24½cm (40 x 9½in), two pieces
Ivory grosgrain elastic, 26cm (10½in), 1½cm (⅝in) wide

Veil (pattern page 121)

Ivory, fine tulle 80 x 35cm (31½ x 14in)
Ivory grosgrain ribbon, 38cm (15in), 2cm (¾in) wide
Large flower
Small velvet flowers x 4
Lace, scrap
Mother-of-pearl beads and seed beads
Small transparent press stud

Pumps (pattern page 119)

Ivory silk, 35 x 10cm (14 x 4in)
Adhesive webbing, 35 x 10cm (14 x 4in)
Ivory, satin cord, 30cm (12in)

Bouquet

Velvet leaves in different shades of green x 4
Flowers in pink and white fabric and velvet x 12
Ivory, fine tulle, 20 x 5cm (8 x 2in)
Ivory satin ribbon, 50cm (20in), 5mm (¼in) wide

Equipment

Pins
Sewing needles
Tacking thread
White sewing thread

DRESS

1 Enlarge the pattern pieces by 140% and cut them out: a half-back, half-front and sleeve for the bodice of the dress.

2 Cut a piece of the poplin measuring 57 x 24cm (22½ x 9½in) for the skirt. Fold the rest of the fabric in half in the direction of the grain and pin on the half-back and half-front, with the latter piece positioned on the fold. Cut the fabric allowing for a 1cm (½in) allowance for the seams and the neckline. Cut one front and two half-backs in the silk in the same way for the lining.

3 Cut a piece of lace 57 x 24cm (22½ x 9½in) for the skirt. Fold the remainder of the lace in half, pin on the pattern for the sleeves and cut, allowing a 1cm (½in) seam allowance all around. Turn the fabric under twice at the top and bottom of the sleeves and stitch to form two channels. Thread 6cm (2½in) of flat elastic through the top channel, and attach it to either side in the seam allowances. Do the same at the bottom with a piece of elastic 11cm (4¼in) long.

4 Join the sleeves to the armholes of the back and front of the bodice, and fold the seam allowances over towards the bodice. Pin the lining on to the front and the back, right sides together, and stitch along the neckline and the opening at the back.

5 Turn right side out and iron, then sew the heart to the front of the bodice. Stitch along the sides of the bodice and the underneath of the sleeves.

6 Join the sides of the lining together. Turn the lining under and tack at the armholes, sewing the turnbacks on to the poplin by hand. Oversew the waist.

7 Fold the rectangle of poplin for the skirt in half, right sides together, and stitch leaving an opening of 5cm (2in) at the top. Repeat with the lace. Oversew the two sides of the openings and iron them over to the reverse.

Place the two skirts on top of one another and tack them together. Run a gathering thread along the top through the two layers and gather the waist of the skirt to that of the bodice. Tack the bodice and the skirt together and stitch. Turn under the lining of the bodice over the top of the gathers and stitch. Attach the satin cord to one side of the back to make four button loops and sew the buttons opposite.

9 Sew a small piece of lace around the waist of the skirt by hand. Hem the bottom of the poplin skirt and stitch a small piece of lace. Finally, hem the lace skirt.

UNDERSKIRT

1 Place the two rectangles of tulle on top of one another and run a gathering thread at the top to adjust the size to 30cm (12in).

2 Pin the grosgrain ribbon to the waist, stretching it out, and sew using a zigzag stitch. Fold the underskirt in half, right sides together, and stitch to close it up.

VEIL

1 Enlarge the pattern for the veil by 200% and cut out. Fold the tulle in half and pin the pattern on top. Cut out close to the edge of the pattern.

2 Gather the top of the veil and adjust its width to 6cm (2½in). Turn the fabric at the ends of some grosgrain ribbon under by ½cm (¼in) and stitch.

3 Fold the grosgrain ribbon in half along the length, slip the top of the veil between the two thicknesses of grosgrain ribbon, centring it well, and stitch the grosgrain ribbon along the length.

4 Sew the large flower to the centre, topped with a pearl bead. Surround with two velvet flowers, mother-of-pearl beads and seed beads.

5 Cut out two motifs from the lace and sew them either side of the large flower on the headband. Sew the press stud to the ends of the grosgrain ribbon.

PUMPS

1 Enlarge the two pattern pieces for the pump by 140% and cut them out. Pin the pieces to the ivory silk, then cut the fabric out, allowing an 8mm (⅜in) allowance all around.

2 Iron on the adhesive webbing to the back of each piece and cut round, following the outlines. Turn under the fabric at the top of the uppers of the pumps and stitch.

3 Close up the upper of the pump. Open out the seam, tack on the sole lining up the middle, aligned with the middle of the upper, then stitch by machine. Trim the silk to 3mm (⅛in) from the seam and turn out the pump.

4 Make the second pump in the same way. Tie two bows with the satin cord and attach them centrally to the front of the pumps.

BOUQUET

1 Place the leaves around the flowers, then wrap the strip of tulle around the stems. Tie the satin ribbon with a pretty bow to hold the bouquet in place.

DOLL WITH STARS

 DOLL WITH STARS

Materials

Dress (pattern page 124)

Star print, beige cotton, one fat quarter
Beige tape, 17cm (6½in)
Beige ric rac, 55cm (21½in)
White mother-of-pearl button with
2 holes, 8mm (⅛in) diameter

Pinafore (see Templates p130/131))

Blue printed cotton, 30 x 30cm (12 x 12in)
Blue striped cotton, 15 x 35cm (6 x 14in)
Flat elastic, 9cm (3½), 5mm (¼in) wide, two pieces
Small wooden heart buttons x 2
Striped fabric, 9 x 9cm (3½ x 3½in), two pieces
DMC Mouliné Stranded Cotton 321 (red) and 822 (beige)

Shoes (see Templates p118)

Brown felt, 15 x 35cm (6 x 14in)
Wooden buttons with 4 holes, 1cm (½in) wide x 2
Brown hook and loop fastening

Equipment

Pins
Sewing and embroidery needles
White, blue and brown sewing thread

Quest for a Cure

DRESS

1 Enlarge the pattern pieces for the dress by 140% and cut out the pieces: two half-sleeves, a half-back and half-front.

2 Fold the fabric in half in the direction of the grain and pin on the pattern pieces. Position the half-sleeves and half-front on the fold. Cut the fabric allowing for a 1cm (½in) seam allowance and 2cm (¾in) for the hems.

3 Join the two half-backs and the front along the shoulder seams, then oversew. Make a box pleat 1½cm (⅝in) at the centre of the neckline and sew it on the reverse for a length of 3cm (1¼in).

4 Insert the sleeves into the armholes, sew them, then close up the sleeves and the sides. Join the two half-backs, leaving an opening of 10cm (4in) at the top. Stitch a 1cm (½in) hem around this. Oversew all the seams.

5 Cut the tape in half along its length and oversew one of the pieces by machine. Sew this piece of tape around the neckline on the right side, turn over then machine stitch close to the edge of the neckline on either side, having turned under a small amount of fabric.

6 Finish the sleeves and the bottom of the dress with a hem, then sew the ric rac at the bottom on the reverse, allowing it to show below slightly. Sew a white button at the top of the opening at the back, and a button loop opposite.

PINAFORE

1 Enlarge the pattern pieces for the pinafore by 140%, and cut them out: a half-back and half-front. Fold the blue printed cotton in half, in the direction of the grain and pin the two pattern pieces to it, along the fold. Cut the fabric, allowing for a 1cm (½in) seam allowance and 2cm (¾in) for the hems.

2 Trace the patterns for the straps (one piece) and the frills (two pieces) in the same way. Fold the fabric in half and pin on the pattern for the straps, remembering to allow a 1cm (½in) seam allowance all around, and pin on the two patterns for the frills, along the fold, lining them up with the grain. This way, the stripes on the straps and the frills are not running in the same direction.

3 Join the sides of the pinafore as far as the armholes, then finish with a hem either side of the armholes. Stitch a channel, 1cm (½in) wide at the top of the back and the front, pass a piece of elastic through each to adjust the width to 9cm (3½in) and sew a few little stitches either side to attach the elastic.

4 Hem the frills, then gather them up on one side, and turn the fabric under along one of the lengths of the straps. Attach the frilled sides onto the fabric that has been turned under, starting and finishing 4½cm (1¾in) from the ends of the straps. Attach the width of the frills to the straps, so that the frills end at a slant. Fold the straps in half, wrong sides together, turn the fabric under on the side without a frill and stitch all the layers together. Turn the fabric under at each end and close using little stitches. Slip the straps to the inside of the pinafore and attach them to the bottom of the armholes and the top of the pinafore, using a few stitches by hand. Sew a little decorative button on the front, level with the channel, on each strap.

5 Stitch a hem at the tops of the pockets and sew them using large running stitches with two strands of red stranded cotton (floss). Place the pockets on the front of the pinafore, turn under the fabric all around and attach using large running stitches with two strands of beige stranded cotton (floss). Sew a 1½cm (⅝in) hem at the bottom of the pinafore, then go back over it using large running stitches with two strands of red stranded cotton (floss).

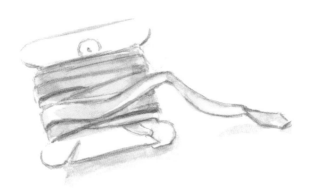

SHOES

1 Enlarge the three pattern pieces for the shoe by 140% and cut them out. Pin the pattern pieces to the felt and cut out, leaving an 8mm (3/8in) seam allowance, except for the strap and the opening, which are cut level with the edge.

2 Topstitch the opening, then close up the upper of the shoe with a seam. Open out the seam, tack on the sole lining up the middle of the sole with the middle of the upper, then stitch by machine. Trim the felt to 3mm (1/8in) from the seam and turn out the shoe.

3 Topstitch around the strap, and sew it to the inside of the shoe, 2½cm (1in) from the back seam. Sew a piece of brown hook and loop fastening to the end of the strap, on the inside, and attach a decorative wooden button on top. Sew the other part of the fastening to the shoe, also 2½cm (1in) from the seam.

4 Make the second shoe in the same way, reversing the position of the strap and fastening.

DOLL WITH STRAWBERRIES

DOLL WITH STRAWBERRIES

Materials

Dress (see Templates p132)

Spotty blue cotton, one fat quarter
White lace, 55cm (21½in), ½cm (¼in) wide
Small mother-of-pearl button
DMC Mouliné Stranded Cotton, white

Hat (see Templates p133)

Spotty cotton, one fat quarter
Striped cotton, one fat quarter
Adhesive webbing, 55 x 70cm (21½ x 27½in)
Pink grosgrain ribbon, 70cm (27½in), ½cm (¼in) wide

Pinafore (see Templates p131)

Liberty print cotton, one fat quarter
Fuchsia pink lace, 70cm (27½in), 1cm (½in) wide
Small flower buttons x 2
Small mother-of-pearl button
DMC Mouliné Stranded Cotton, white

Espadrilles (see Templates p118)

Pink linen, 25 x 5cm (10 x 2in)
Natural linen, 15 x 5cm (6 x 2in)
Light beige felt, 25 x 8cm (10 x 3¼in)
Adhesive webbing, 40 x 5cm (16 x 2in)
Pink ribbon, 110cm (43in), ½cm (⅝in) wide
DMC Mouliné Stranded Cotton, white

Equipment

Pins
Sewing and embroidery needles
Beige, red, blue and pink sewing thread

DRESS

1 Enlarge the two pattern pieces by 140% and cut them out: a half-back and half-front. Fold the fabric in half in the direction of the grain and pin the two pattern pieces on, with the half-front positioned on the fold.

2 Cut the pieces out, allowing for a 1cm (½in) seam allowance and 2cm (¾in) for the hems.

3 Place the two half-backs together, right sides together, and stitch the centre back as far as the bottom of the opening. Open out the seam, mark a turnback either side of the opening and stitch.

4 Join the back and front along the shoulders and iron the seams out flat. Hem around the neckline and armholes before hand stitching lace around these hems.

5 Close up the sides of the dress by machine and hem the bottom. Sew a small white button at the top of the opening at the back and sew a button loop opposite with the embroidery yarn.

HAT

1 Enlarge the pattern pieces by 140% and cut them out: a crown and straight edge for the sides of the hat, a rounded front brim and rounded back brim.

2 Position the pattern pieces on the spotty fabric, following the grain as indicated (the two straight sides of the hat are cut on the bias, the centre back and front of the rounded brims are on the grain). Cut out the pieces allowing for a 1cm (½in) seam allowance. Do the same with the striped fabric. Iron some adhesive webbing to the back of each piece and trim.

3 Place the spotty straight edges together, right sides together, and join the sides to close up. Iron the seams out flat. Pin these edges to the bottom of the spotty hat, by lining up the notches, and stitch. Place the two spotty rounded brims together, right sides together, and join the sides to close up. Iron the seams out flat. Pin these edges to the sides of the hat, by lining up the notches, and stitch.

4 Join the striped lining of the hat in the same way, leaving an opening in one seam for turning the hat right side out. Place the outside of the hat and its lining together, right sides together, lining up the seams, and stitch along the edge. Turn right side out at the opening and close the opening by hand, using little stitches. Iron the whole hat, exterior and lining, and sew a line of topstitching 1mm (¹⁄₁₆in) from the edge.

5 Cut 2½cm (1in) of grosgrain ribbon and sew it to one side of the hat, on a straight edge, to form a loop. Position the rest of the grosgrain ribbon on the hat, slipping it into the loop, and close it up with a pretty bow on the other side.

PINAFORE

1 Enlarge the two pattern pieces by 140% and cut them out: a half-back/front for the yoke and strap. Fold the fabric in half in the direction of the grain and pin the two pattern pieces to it, with the half-back/front positioned on the fold.

2 Cut out the pieces, allowing for a 1cm (½in) seam allowance and 2cm (¾in) for the hems. Cut out a rectangle 70 x 19cm (27½ x 7½in) for the bottom of the pinafore. Turn under the fabric at the top of the yoke and on the sides of the back opening, and stitch. Gather the large rectangle of fabric, leaving the seam allowance free, so that it is adjusted to the size of the yoke. Then pin the top to the bottom of the pinafore and stitch.

3 Fold the pinafore in half, right sides together, and stitch to close it up, from the bottom of the pinafore to the bottom of the yoke. Iron to open the seam.

4 Fold the straps in half, right sides together, and stitch leaving one end open. Turn out and iron. Position the straps on the front and back of the pinafore and sew in place.

5 Sew a white button at the top of the opening at the back and a button loop opposite with the embroidery yarn. Stitch flower buttons at the level of the straps on the front. Hem at the bottom of the pinafore and sew on the lace by hand, 2cm (¾in) from the edge.

ESPADRILLES

1 Enlarge the three pattern pieces by 140% and cut them out: a sole, upper and heel. Cut four soles in the felt, two uppers in the pink linen and two heels in the natural linen. Cut close to the edge of the patterns.

2 Place the soles together, in pairs, and stitch them 1mm (⅟₁₆in) from the edge. Iron some adhesive webbing to the back of the heel and the upper of the espadrilles and trim following the outlines. Close up the dart on the upper, and topstitch all these pieces 1mm (⅟₁₆in) from the edge.

3 Pin the uppers and the heels to the soles, with the wrong side of these pieces against the inside of the soles, and stitch along the edge. Embroider around the edge of the espadrilles and the tip of the upper, at the centre using blanket stitch.

4 Cut two pieces of ribbon, 4cm (1½in) long, fold them in half and sew them underneath the upper of the espadrilles, in the centre, leaving a loop of ribbon showing. Thread 50cm (20in) of ribbon through each loop and, with a large needle, pierce the natural linen back of the espadrilles and thread the ribbon through. Make the second espadrille in the same way.

BEDTIME
DOLL

 BEDTIME DOLL

Materials

Nightdress (see Templates p124)

Red and white star print cotton, one fat quarter
Broderie anglaise lace, 75cm (29½in), 1½cm (⅝in) wide
Red satin ribbon, 30cm (12in), 3mm (⅛in) wide
White tape, 20cm (8in)
Thin elastic, 20cm (8in)
Small, white, mother of pearl star button with 2 holes
Small, white, mother of pearl button
with 2 holes, 8mm (⅜in) diameter
DMC Mouliné Stranded Cotton 304 (red)

Teddy (see Templates p75/p130)

Beige linen, 16 x 35cm (6¼ x 14in)
Red and white star print cotton, 9 x 18cm (3½ x 7in)
Polyester wadding (batting)
DMC Mouliné Stranded Cotton 304 (red),
844 (brown) and 3031 (grey)
Embroidered label

Cushion

Red and white striped cotton, one fat quarter
Red cotton ribbon, 30cm (12in), ½cm (¼in) wide
Red felt, scrap
Polyester wadding (batting)
DMC Mouliné Stranded Cotton 304 (red) and ecru

Dressing gown (see Templates p134)

White linen, 25 x 66cm (10 x 26in)
White broderie anglaise, 70cm (27½in), 2cm (¾in) wide
Red and white star print cotton, one fat quarter
Red satin ribbon, 5cm (2in), 3mm (⅛in) wide
DMC Mouliné Stranded Cotton, white

Mules (see Templates p119)

White felt, 14 x 26cm (5½ x 10½in)
Small, white pom poms x 2
DMC Mouliné Stranded Cotton 304 (red)

Equipment

Sewing and embroidery needles
White and beige sewing thread
Pinking shears
Crochet hook

NIGHTDRESS

1 Enlarge the pattern pieces for the nightdress by 140%, and cut them out: two half-sleeves, a half-back and half-front.

2 Fold the fabric in half in the direction of the grain and pin on the patterns. The half-f ront and half-sleeves are positioned on the fold. Cut the fabric allowing for a 1cm (½in) seam allowance and 2cm (¾in) for the hems. Mark the notches with some pins.

3 Join the two half-backs and the front along the shoulder seams, then oversew. Make a box pleat of 1½cm (⅝in) at the centre of the neckline and sew it on the reverse for a length of 3cm (1¼in). Gather the sleeves between the notches, tack them to the armholes and stitch. Fold the sleeves in half, right sides together, sew a line of stitching along the sleeves and the sides.

4 Fold over the ends of the sleeves by 2½cm (1in), turn a small amount of fabric under and stitch along the edge of the fabric all the way around, leaving a little opening so that you can thread the elastic through. Sew a second, parallel line of stitching at 5mm (¼in) all the

way around. Thread 10cm (4in) of thin elastic into each channel and tie the ends together. Join the two half-backs with a seam, leaving an opening of 10cm (4in) at the top. Oversew all the seams. Turn the nightdress right side out.

5 Cut the tape in half along its length and oversew one of the pieces by machine. Tack some lace and the piece of oversewn tape around the neckline, on the right side of the fabric. Turn the tape to the inside of the neckline and topstitch along the neckline.

6 Sew a 1cm (½in) hem either side of the opening for the back. Stitch a little white button at the top of this opening, using red stranded cotton, and sew a button loop opposite, also in red stranded cotton (floss).

7 Finish the bottom of the skirt with a hem, and stitch white lace to it, so that the broderie anglaise shows below. Sew a decorative bow in red ribbon just above the box pleat, with a star button sewn on top using red stranded cotton (floss).

TEDDY

1 Enlarge the pattern for the teddy by 140% and make two copies. Cut out these two pieces. Fold the fabric in half, in the direction of the grain, and pin on the two pieces, along the fold. Cut out the fabric adding 1cm (½in) all around.

2 Place the two pieces of fabric together and sew a line of stitching all the way around, leaving an opening of 3cm (1¼in) on one side. Trim the fabric to 5mm (¼in) from the seam and turn the fabric right side out. Fill with wadding (batting) and close the opening with little hand stitches.

3 Embroider the face by sewing a cross in each ear with one strand of brown stranded cotton (floss). The nose and the mouth are made with two strands of brown stranded cotton (floss): a triangle that points

downwards, with an arrow below it that also points downwards. The two eyes are made from little circles, embroidered using stem stitch with two strands of grey stranded cotton (floss).

4 Trim the top of the star fabric using pinking shears. Make two openings inside, 3½cm (1in) long, to insert the arms of the teddy, 2cm (¾in) from the top and at 4½cm (1¾in) from the sides.

5 Fold the fabric in half, right sides together, and close the back with a line of stitching. Turn the fabric under by 1cm (½in) at the bottom and sew it using a large running stitch by hand with two strands of red stranded cotton (floss). Turn the fabric right side out and gather the top of the blouse using six strands of red stranded cotton (floss), and tie around the neck of the teddy.

CUSHION

1 Cut out two 18½cm (7in) squares from the fabric. Place them right sides together, and stitch all around, 1cm (½in) from the edge, leaving an opening on one side. Turn cover out.

2 Sew a red felt heart in the middle of the cushion cover using two strands of ecru stranded cotton (floss). Embroider a red star either side of this heart with six strands of red stranded cotton (floss).

3 Fill the cushion with wadding (batting) and close up the opening using little hand stitches. Embroider a line of large running stitches all around the cushion using two strands of red stranded cotton (floss). Tie a decorative bow with ribbon and attach it to the top left corner of the cushion.

DRESSING GOWN

1 Enlarge the pattern pieces by 140% and cut them out: a half-back, half-front, half-sleeve and half-waistband. Fold the fabric in half in the direction of the grain and pin on the pattern pieces. The half-back, half-sleeve and half-waistband are positioned on the fold. Cut the fabric, allowing for a 1cm (½in) seam allowance and 2cm (¾in) for the hems.

2 Join the back and fronts along the shoulder seams, then sew the sleeves to the armholes. Stitch the side seams and underneath the sleeves.

3 Tack broderie anglaise to the reverse, around the opening of the dressing gown (down the fronts and around the neckline), and stitch by machine. Pin a hem at the ends of the sleeves and at the bottom of the dressing gown and stitch by machine.

4 Place the linen strip for the waistband and the star print cotton together, right sides together, and stitch leaving one end open. Trim the fabric to 5mm (¼in) from the seams and turn right side out. Turn the fabric under around the opening and close by hand.

5 Make two chains, 2cm (¾in) long, with the crochet hook and embroidery thread, and sew them to the side seams to make the loops for the waistband. Turn under the ends of the satin ribbon and sew it inside the dressing gown, at the centre of the back neckline.

MULES

1 Enlarge the pattern pieces by 140% and cut them out: four soles and two uppers. Pin the pattern pieces to the felt, then cut out close to the edge for the two uppers, leaving a 1cm (½in) seam allowance for the soles.

2 Mark the centre notches on the soles and uppers with some pins, then place the soles together in pairs lining up the notches. Tack the soles. Arrange the uppers on the soles lining up the notches and tack. Sew a line of stitching all the way around then trim the fabric to 2mm (¹⁄₁₆in) from the line of stitching. Make the second mule in the same way.

3 Embroider the uppers of the mules with a line of running stitch along the opening using two strands of red stranded cotton (floss). Embroider three stars on each upper forming a triangle pointing downwards using three strands of red stranded cotton (floss). Sew a little white pompom between the two stars at the top.

DOLL IN
BLUE

 DOLL IN BLUE

Materials

Blouse [see Templates p135]

White poplin, one fat quarter
White tape, 15cm (6in)
Thin elastic, 20cm (8in)
White flower in guipure lace
White mother-of-pearl button, 8mm (⅜in) diameter

Pinafore dress [see Templates p125]

Blue and white hound's tooth checked
cotton, one fat quarter
White mother-of-pearl buttons with 4
holes, 12mm (½in) diameter x 3
Grey hook and loop fastening
DMC Mouliné Stranded Cotton 321 (red)

Shoes [see Templates p118]

Brown felt, 15 x 35cm (6 x 14in)
Wooden buttons with 4 holes, 1cm (½in) wide x 2
Brown hook and loop fastening

Satchel

Brown felt, 13 x 38cm (5 x 15in)
Camel cotton ribbon, 60cm (23½in), 1cm (½in) wide
Buckle
Brown hook and loop fastening

Equipment

Sewing and embroidery needles
Blue, white and brown sewing thread
Flax string

BLOUSE

1 Enlarge the pattern pieces by 140%, and cut the pieces out: a half-back, half-front, sleeve and two half-collars.

2 Fold the fabric in half in the direction of the grain and pin on the pattern pieces. Only the centre of the half-front is positioned on the fold. Cut the fabric allowing for a 1cm (½in) seam allowance and 2cm (¾in) for the hems. Using some pins, mark on the fabric the notches for the gathers and the centre of the sleeves.

3 Join the two half-backs and the front along the shoulder seams, then stitch and oversew. Gather the sleeves between notches A and B and attach them to the armholes by lining up the notches. Fold the sleeves in half, right sides together, sew a line of stitching along the sleeves and sides and oversew.

4 Turn under the ends of the sleeves by 2½cm (1in), turn a small amount of fabric under and stitch along the edge of the fabric all the way around, leaving a little opening so that you can thread the elastic through. Sew a second, parallel line of stitching, at 5mm (⅝in), all around. Thread 10cm (4in) of thin elastic through each channel and tie the ends together. Turn the sleeves right side out.

5 Position two half-collars right sides together and stitch along the straight side and the outer rounded edge. Turn this half-collar out and mark notch C with a pin. Make up the other half-collar in the same way.

6 Place the two half-collars on the neckline lining up the notches with the fabric right side out. Place a piece of tape on top and tack. Sew a line of stitching, trim the tape to 3mm (⅛in) from the seam, then turn it over to the reverse of the bodice. Attach the tape to the shoulder seams with a few little hand stitches.

7 Hem along the two overlaps at the back and along the bottom of the blouse. Sew a little white button at the top of the opening of one of the back pieces, sew a button loop on the other piece opposite. To finish, sew a little white flower in guipure lace on to the front of the blouse, at the centre.

PINAFORE DRESS

1 Enlarge the pattern pieces by 140% and cut the pieces out: a bib, strap, half-waistband, half-back and half-front. Fold the hound's tooth fabric in half, in the direction of the grain, and pin on the pattern pieces. The half-back and half-front are positioned against the fold, along with the waistband. Cut the fabric allowing for a 1cm (½in) seam allowance and 2cm (¾in) for the hems.

2 Tack six flat pleats around the back and front of the skirt, as indicated on the pattern. Place the back and front right sides together, and stitch the sides. End the seam 6cm (2½in) from the top on one of the sides to keep an opening. Sew a hem at the bottom.

3 Fold the straps in half along the length and stitch a line along two sides, turning them out. Place the two pieces for the bib on top of one another, right sides together. Slip the two straps between these two pieces. Stitch the side of the bib where the open ends of the straps are located, then the two sides. Turn the bib right side out.

4 Place the bib on the front of the skirt and tack the bottom of the bib to the pleats. Tack the bottom of the waistband to the skirt, right sides together, catching the bottom of the bib between the waistband and the skirt. Stitch everything together, close the sides of the waistband and turn out. Turn under the fabric on the other side and stitch to the reverse of the skirt.

5 Sew a white button to one of the ends of the waistband of the skirt using two strands of red stranded cotton (floss), and sew a red button loop opposite on the other end. Sew the other two buttons to the bottom of the bib, catching the waistband in at the same time. Sew a line of cross stitches along the top of the bib, using two strands red stranded cotton (floss). Sew a piece of hook and loop fastening at the bottom of each strap, and two other pieces opposite on the inside of the waistband at the back.

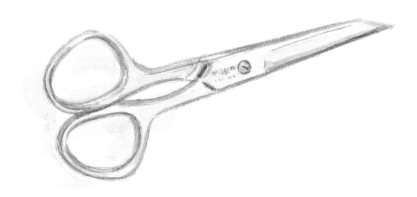

SHOES

1 Enlarge the three pattern pieces for the shoe by 140% and cut the pieces out. Pin the pattern pieces to the felt, then cut the fabric out, leaving an 8mm (⅜in) seam allowance, except for the strap and the opening, which are cut level with the edge.

2 Oversew the opening, then close up the upper of the shoe with a seam. Open out the seam, tack on the sole lining up the middle of the sole with the middle of the upper, then stitch by machine. Trim the felt to 3mm (⅛in) from the seam and turn out the shoe.

3 Oversew around the strap, and sew it to the inside of the shoe, 2½cm (1in) from the back seam. Sew a piece of brown hook and loop fastening to the end of the strap on the inside, and attach a little wooden decorative button on top. Sew the other part of the fastening to the shoe, also 2½cm (1in) from the seam.

4 Make the second shoe in the same way, reversing the position of the strap and fastening.

SATCHEL

1 Cut one rectangle, 13 x 29½cm (5 x 11½in), and two rectangles, 4 x 8½cm (1½ x 3¼in), from the felt.

2 Fold over the left part of the large felt rectangle and tack the little rectangles at the top and bottom to form the sides, leaving a flap 8½cm (3in) wide on the right. Tack the felt wrong sides together. Stitch the seams on the right side and topstitch around the flap, as well as the top of the pocket of the satchel.

3 Cut a piece of camel ribbon 12cm (4½in) long and turn under 1cm (½in) on either side. Attach this ribbon to the top of the flap to make a handle by stitching a square over the two pieces that are turned under using some brown sewing thread.

4 Cut a piece of camel ribbon 34cm (13½in) long. Fold it in half, making a point in the fold.

Stitch this point in the ribbon centrally at the top of the back of the satchel with some brown sewing thread. Attach each of the ends to the bottom, on the seams, also with some brown sewing thread.

5 Secure a piece of brown hook and loop fastening at the centre of the pocket, 3cm (1¼in) from the top, and the other part to the inside of the flap, 1cm (½in) from the edge.

6 Thread a piece of camel ribbon, 9cm (3½in) long, through the buckle. Leave one end hanging by 2½cm (1in) underneath the buckle, folding the other around the bar at the top.

7 Sew a line of stitching just above this bar with some flax string sewing thread and attach the ribbon to the flap by stitching along the lower line of stitching for the hook and loop fastening with brown sewing thread. Embroider around the flap in a running stitch using flax string along the line of machine stitching.

BALLERINA DOLL

 BALLERINA DOLL

Materials

Tutu (see Templates p137)

Star print cambric, one fat quarter
Round elastic, 20cm (8in)
Small hotfix rhinestone beads x 15

Underskirt (see Templates p136)

Pink tulle, 75 x 25cm (29½ x 10in)
Round elastic, 20cm (8in)

Tiara

Silver pipe-cleaner, 50cm (20in) long
Silver elastic yarn
Teardrop rhinestone bead

Leotard (see Templates p131)

Pink star print cambric, one fat quarter
Pink cambric, one fat quarter
Silver lace, 10cm (4in), 1cm (½in) wide
Fuchsia pink satin ribbon, 12cm (4½in), 5mm (¼in) wide
2 plastic press studs
Hotfix star

Shrug

Silver-grey wool
Mother-of-pearl star button

Ballet shoes (see Templates p119)

Pink silk, 35 x 10cm (14 x 4in)
Adhesive webbing, 35 x 10cm (14 x 4in)
Pink satin ribbon, 140cm (55in), 5mm (¼in) wide

Barrel bag (see Templates p131/137)

Light pink, star print cambric, one fat quarter
White cotton, 36 x 15cm (14 x 6in)
Iron-on wadding (batting), 36 x 15cm
(14 x 6in), 5mm (¼in) wide
Grey serge ribbon, 75cm (29½in), 1cm (½in) wide
Zip, 13cm (5in) long

Equipment

Pins
Sewing needle
Tacking thread
Dark pink and light pink sewing thread
3.5mm (US4) knitting needles

TUTU

1 Enlarge the pattern by 120% and cut it out. Fold the cambric in half in the direction of the grain and pin the pattern on top, with the centre front positioned on the fold.

2 Cut the fabric, allowing a 1cm (½in) seam allowance for the back seam and the channel at the waist and 2cm (¾in) for the hem at the bottom. Close up the back of the tutu, then oversew the seam and iron it open.

3 Fold over 5mm (¼in) at the waist, leaving a little opening. Thread the elastic cord through this channel and gather the waist to a length of 18cm (7in), tying the two ends of elastic. Hem the bottom edge.

4 Glue the hotfix rhinestone beads onto the front of the tutu, scattering them like a starry sky.

UNDERSKIRT

1 Enlarge the pattern by 120% and cut out. Fold the tulle in half and pin the pattern on top, with the centre front and back positioned on the fold.

2 Cut the tulle, allowing a 1cm (½in) seam allowance around the waist. Cut a second circle of tulle in the same way.

3 Place the two circles of tulle on top of one another, fold over 5mm (¼in) at the waist and stitch, leaving a little opening. Thread elastic cord through this channel and gather the waist to 18cm (7in), tying the two ends of elastic.

TIARA

1 Cut a 26cm (10½in) piece from the pipe-cleaner. Fold it in half, bending the ends around to form a ring. This will be the lower part of the tiara.

2 Cut another piece of pipe-cleaner, 20cm (8in) long and make three spirals to form the top part of the tiara. Attach this top part to the lower part, at the centre, by twisting it around either side.

3 Stitch the rhinestone bead to the centre of the top part, so that it hangs down. Connect the two rings of the lower portion with some elastic yarn.

LEOTARD

1 Enlarge the pattern by 120% and cut it out. Fold the star print cambric in half in the direction of the grain and pin the pattern on top, with the centre front along the fold.

2 Cut the fabric, allowing a 1cm (½in) seam allowance all around. Do the same with the plain cambric.

3 Cut the ribbon in half and pin the ends of each piece to the reverse of the plain fabric, at the level of the straps (with the straps against the fabric and the ends lined up with the edge of the fabric).

4 Place the two fabrics together, right sides together, and stitch all around leaving an opening in a seam at the centre back. Turn right side out, iron and close the opening.

5 Place the bottoms of the two back parts together, hold them together with two little stitches and sew one side of a press stud on top. Sew the other part of the press stud at the front crotch, on the plain lining.

6 Make a small pleat at the top of the leotard, at the centre of the front, and secure with a little stitch. Sew the lace along the neckline. Sew on another press stud to close the top at the back. Attach the hotfix star to the centre of the neckline.

SHRUG

This is knitted in a single piece and starts at the bottom of the back.

Cast on 29 sts and work in stocking (stockinette) st for 11 rows (3cm/1¼in).

Shape the sleeves by casting on 18 sts at the beginning of the next 2 rows. 65 sts.

Continue in stocking (stockinette) stitch until the piece measures 7cm (2¾in) ending on a purl row.

Next row: K27, cast (bind) off next 11 sts, k to end.

Complete the left side of the shrug on these last 27 sts as follows:

Increase 1 st at neck edge on next row. 28 sts.

Work 3 rows without shaping.

Repeat the last four rows three more times. 31 sts.

AT THE SAME TIME when the piece measures 13cm (5in) cast (bind) off the 18 sts for the sleeve at the beginning of the next purl row.

When the work measures 15cm (6in) increase 1 st at neck edge on next 5 alternate rows.

Continue without shaping until work measures 17cm (6½in).

Cast (bind) off the remaining 18 sts.

Rejoin yarn to the remaining 27 sts and complete as for the left side but reversing the shaping.

Fold the shrug in half and close up the sides and the sleeves. Sew a little button on to one front piece and sew a button loop opposite.

BALLET SHOES

1 Enlarge the two pattern pieces by 120% and cut them out. Pin the pieces to the ivory silk, then cut the fabric out, allowing an 8mm (⅜in) seam allowance all around.

2 Iron some adhesive webbing to the back of each piece and trim, following the outlines. Oversew the opening, then close the upper of the shoe with a seam. Open out the seam, tack on the sole, lining up the middle of the

sole with the middle of the upper, then machine stitch. Trim the fabric to 3mm (⅛in) from the seam and turn out the shoe.

3 Make the second shoe in the same way.

4 Cut the ribbon into four and attach two pieces of ribbon to the inside of each shoe, at the back.

BARRELL BAG

1 Enlarge the two pattern pieces by 120% and cut them out. Pin the pieces on to the cambric allowing for a 1cm (½in) seam allowance.

2 Using the two pattern pieces, cut out a rectangle and two circles from the wadding (batting), without seam allowances, and iron them on to the pink cambric.

3 Pin the zip to the reverse of the rectangle of fabric, along the opening of the bag, and stitch. Cut 65cm (25½in) of serge ribbon and position it on the bag to form handles of equal length, starting at the centre fold, at the base.

4 Stitch the handles either side of the serge ribbon, starting at the bottom of the bag. Cut two pieces of serge ribbon, 4cm (1½in) long, fold them in half and pin them either side of the zip.

5 Tack the circles to the sides of the cambric, then stitch them by hand. Cut the lining from the cotton, 5mm (¼in) smaller than the bag and assemble it. Slip the lining inside the bag, turn a small amount of fabric under along the opening and sew it to the inside edges of the zip.

DOLL IN A RAINCOAT

 DOLL IN A RAINCOAT

Materials

Raincoat (see Templates p138)
Canvas, 35 x 60cm (14 x 23½in)
Press stud x 1
Metal button

Sailor's top (see Templates p139)
Striped cotton, one fat quarter
White broderie anglaise, 35cm (14in), 7cm (2¾in) wide
Grey, star-shaped, mother-of-pearl buttons x 2
Small white button
Red lace, 21cm (8¼in), 1cm (½in) wide
DMC Mouliné Stranded Cotton, white

Trousers (see Templates p139)
Dark grey linen, 50 x 40cm (20 x 16in)
Flat elastic, 26cm (10½in), 1cm (½in) wide
Grey mother-of-pearl button

Cap
Small ball of navy blue and grey cotton yarn
Small ball of fine silver cotton yarn
Star charm
Safety pin

Boots (see Templates p118/p119)
Canvas, 40 x 20cm (16 x 8in)
Red felt, 15 x 10cm (6 x 4in)

Equipment
Pins
Sewing and embroidery needles
4mm (US6) knitting needles
Red, white and blue sewing thread

RAINCOAT

1 Enlarge the pattern pieces by 140% and cut them out: a half-hood, half-back, half-front, pocket and sleeve. Fold the canvas in half and pin the pieces on, with the centre back positioned on the fold.

2 Cut the canvas, allowing for a 1cm (½in) seam allowance and 2cm (¾in) for the hems and around the hood.

3 Place the two pieces for the hood together and stitch to close them up. Turn under 2cm (¾in) of fabric all around the opening and stitch. Join the back and fronts along the shoulders. Fold the facings in half for the fronts, right sides together, stitch the top and turn right side out.

4 Cut notches around the armhole and join the sleeves to the body. Then sew the sides and underneath the sleeves. Hem the ends of the sleeves and the bottom of the raincoat. Turn the fabric under by 1cm (½in) at the sides and bottom of the pocket, and fold under 2cm (¾in) at the top and stitch.

5 Stitch the pocket to one front piece, close to the edge of the side seam. Place the press stud at the top of the facing and attach the decorative button.

BOBBLE HAT

Cast on 60 stitches in navy blue. Work 12 rows in stocking (stockinette) stitch in blue, then continue in stocking (stockinette) stitch alternating the colours: 4 rows grey and silver worked together, 4 rows in blue.

Work 24 rows in striped pattern.

Decrease row: K1, *k4, k2tog; repeat from * to last 5 sts, k5. 51 sts.

Work 3 rows without shaping.

Decrease row: K1, *k3, k2tog; repeat from * to last 5 sts, k5. 42 sts.

Work 1 row.

Decrease row: K1, *k2, k2tog; repeat from * to last st, k1. 32 sts.

Work 1 row.

Decrease row: K1, *k1, k2tog; repeat from * to last st, k1. 22 sts.

Work 1 row.

Decrease row: K1, K2tog to last st, k1. 12 sts.

Repeat last row. 7 sts.

Thread a piece of yarn through the remaining stitches, draw up and close the hat at the side seam.

Make a little pompom using the grey cotton mixed with silver, with two 5cm (2in) circles, and sew it to the top of the hat. Attach the charm to the hat with the safety pin.

SAILORS TOP

1 Enlarge the pattern pieces by 140% and cut them out: a half-back, half-front and sleeve. Fold the striped cotton in half, pin the half-back and half-front to the fabric, with this last piece positioned along the fold. Cut the fabric, allowing for a 1cm (½in) seam allowance and 2cm (¾in) for the hems. Cut the sleeves from the lace.

2 Place the two half-backs together, right sides together, and stitch the centre back, leaving an opening of 10cm (4in) at the top. Iron open the seam and mark a turnback either side of the opening, stitching the fabric that has been turned under along the opening.

3 Join the back and front along the shoulders, iron the seams out flat and sew a hem around the neckline.

4 Join the sleeves to the body of the sailor's top, then stitch the sides and underneath the sleeves from the top of the turned under fabric to the ends of the sleeves. Hem around the vents at the sides, then at the bottom of the sailor's top.

5 Stitch the star buttons on the front around the edge of the neckline and the lace, 2cm (¾in) from the bottom. Sew the little white button at the top of the back and sew a button loop opposite with the embroidery yarn.

TROUSERS

1 Enlarge the pattern pieces by 140% and cut them out: a half-back-front, pocket and flap. Fold the fabric in half in the direction of the grain and pin on the different pattern pieces.

2 Cut out the pieces twice, but just one pocket, allowing for a 1cm (½in) seam allowance and 2cm (¾in) for the hems.

3 Place the two parts of the flap for the pocket together, right sides together, and stitch all around leaving an opening. Turn right side out, iron and topstitch 2mm (1⁄16in) from the edge. Turn under 1cm (½in) of fabric at the top of the pocket and stitch.

4 Mark the box pleat using an iron and stitch it for 2cm (¾in), starting at the bottom, and for 1cm (½in), starting from the top. Turn under the seam allowance around the pocket using the iron, then pin the pocket on to the right leg, midway between the front and back, and stitch. Stitch the flap at the top of the pocket, so that it is positioned 1cm (½in) above the pocket. Sew the button to the flap.

5 Stitch the legs of the trousers, then pin the inside leg and stitch. Iron the seam out flat. Turn under the fabric to the reverse along the waist and pin a hem. Stitch, leaving an opening, then thread the elastic through this channel to adjust the waist to 25cm (10in) and sew the two ends together. Hem the bottom of the trousers.

BOOTS

1 Enlarge the pattern pieces by 140% and cut them out: a sole, upper and leg piece. Fold the canvas in half and pin on the leg piece and the upper of the boot. Fold the felt in half and pin on the sole.

2 Cut the pieces, allowing a 1cm (½in) seam allowance all around. Close the front dart in the uppers and then pin the upper to the leg pieces, stitching together. Topstitch 2mm (⅟₁₆in) from the seam.

3 Fold the fabric over at the top of the leg pieces and stitch, then close the back seam of the boots. Join to the soles by lining up the notches back and front. Trim the soles to 3mm (⅛in) from the seam.

4 Make the second boot in the same way. If you want to, you can sew a piece of cord through the top of the boots using a large needle and tie a bow on the front.

FAIRY
DOLLS

 FAIRY DOLLS

Materials

Star dress (see Templates p140)

White star print cambric, one fat quarter
White cambric, 74 x 7cm (29 x 2¾in)
Pink heart button
Flat elastic, 25cm (10in), 3mm (⅛in) wide

Pumps (see Templates)

Pink felt, 35 x 10cm (14 x 4in)
Pink star buttons x 2
Two strands of pearly pink cotton, 15cm (6in) long

Hair clips

Miniature children's hair-clips x 2
Pink fuchsia lace, 40cm (16in), 1cm (½in) wide

Magic wand (see Templates)

Iron-on sequin sheet
Silver fabric, 5cm (2in) square
Silver ribbon, 15cm (6in), 3mm (⅛in) wide
Silver yarn, 25cm (10in)
Fine skewer
Silver elastic, 10cm (4in), 5mm (¼in) wide

Cupcakes (see Templates)

(for 1 cupcake)
Patterned cotton, 14cm (5½in) square
Spotty cotton, 20 x 7cm (8 x 2¾in)
White ric rac, 15cm (6in)
Small red pompom
Synthetic filling

Butterfly wings (see Templates)

White organdie, 30 x 20cm (12 x 8in)
Silver pipe-cleaners, 50cm (20in) long x 2
Fine, round, silver elastic, 34cm (13½in)
DMC Mouliné Stranded Cotton, silver
Hotfix stars x 8

Tablecloth

Floral, spotty and checked fabric
Fine white cotton for lining, 37cm (14½in) square
Liberty print cotton, 20 x 13cm (8 x 5in)
Green felt, scrap

Kimono (see Templates)

Liberty print cotton, one fat quarter
Fuchsia pink grosgrain ribbon, 50cm
(20in), 5mm (¼in) wide
Small mother-of-pearl button
Stranded Cotton, fucshia

Pink shoes (see Templates)

Pink felt, 15 x 35cm (6 x 14in)
Liberty print tape, 18cm (7in), 8mm (⅜in) wide
Small buttons x 2
Small plastic press studs x 2

Equipment

Pins
Sewing and embroidery needles
Pink, white and blue sewing thread
Adhesive

STAR DRESS

1 Enlarge the two pattern pieces by 140%. Cut them out: a half-back and half-front. Fold the fabric in half in the direction of the grain and pin the patterns on top, along the fold. Cut out, allowing for a 1cm (½in) seam allowance and 2cm (¾in) for the hems.

2 Place the back and front together, right sides together, and stitch the sides as far as the ends of the armholes. Iron the seams out flat and sew a little hem around the armholes.

3 Stitch a little hem on a length of the plain fabric to obtain a piece 74 x 3½cm (29in x 1½in), then fold it in half, right sides together, and join the widths to close

them up into a circle. Pin this frill to the top of the dress, arranging the gathers evenly, with the unhemmed side of the frill against the top of the dress, and tack the two thicknesses together.

4 Hem around the neckline with the two fabrics placed together, leaving an opening. Thread the elastic through this hem with a little safety pin to gather the neckline to 24cm (9½in). Sew the two ends of elastic together and close up the opening.

5 Stitch a little hem at the bottom of the dress. Sew the star button on the frill at the front of the dress.

PUMPS

1 Enlarge the two pattern pieces by 140% and cut them out. Pin the pieces to the felt then cut the fabric out, allowing an 8mm (⅜in) allowance, except for the top of the pump, which is cut close to the edge of the pattern.

2 Join the pumps, following the instructions for the shoes on page 30, but without the strap.

3 Tie two little bows with the pearly cotton and attach them to the front of the pumps, at the centre. Sew a little star button just beneath.

CUPCAKES

1 Enlarge the pattern pieces by 140% and cut them out: a top, side and base. Pin the pieces to the fabric (the base and side in the spotty fabric, the top in the patterned fabric) and cut out, allowing a 1cm (½in) seam allowance.

2 Join the top and side of the cupcake, then fold in half, right sides together, and stitch to close up into a circle. Tack to the base and sew.

3 Turn right side out. Run a gathering thread around the top and fill with synthetic filling. Pull the gathering thread gently to close up the cupcake. Sew the ric rac around the cupcake and the pompom on the top. Make the second cupcake in the same way.

MAGIC WAND

1 Enlarge the star pattern by 140% and cut it out. Place this on the sequin sheet, trace its outline with a pencil and cut out.

2 Cut the skewer to 16cm (6¼in) long and place one of its ends on the star, so that it sits in the centre. Position the square of silver fabric on top, protect it all with greaseproof paper and iron to adhere together.

3 Trim the fabric following the outline of the star. Tie the ribbon and silver yarn to the rod, beneath the star. Tie the elastic to the base of the wand to make a bracelet for hanging the wand on the arm of the doll.

BUTTERFLY WINGS

1 Enlarge the pattern by 140% and cut out. Fold the organdie in half, pin the pattern on top and cut out, allowing for a 1cm (½in) seam allowance.

2 Mark a 1cm (½in) turnback to the reverse around each wing using the iron. Place a pipe-cleaner on top, leaving the ends showing by 3cm (1¼in) at the join, and attach everything using zigzag stitch.

3 Bend the ends of the pipe-cleaners together to join the wings to each other. Tie the two ends of elastic, slip the elastic behind the join of the wings, tying a knot to secure.

4 Embroider the arabesques on the wings using tacking stitch with two strands of silver stranded cotton (floss), following the design of the pattern.

5 Attach the stars to the wings using hotfix glue, protecting everything with greaseproof paper to avoid damaging the organdie.

TABLECLOTH

1 Cut out 25 9cm (3½in) squares from the fabrics (these measurements include a 1cm (½in) seam allowance). Join these squares in strips of five and iron the strips to turn under the seams in the same direction.

2 Join the strips to each other to form a large square and fold over the seams in the same direction.

3 Cut a square the same size from the white canvas for the lining. Place the lining and the patchwork together, right sides together, and sew them together all the way around, leaving an opening for turning.

4 Turn out, iron and close the opening using little hand stitches. Topstitch around the tablecloth, 2mm (¹⁄₁₆in) from the edge.

LITTLE FAIRY DOLL

KIMONO

1 Enlarge the pattern pieces by 120% and cut out: a half-front bodice, half-back bodice, half-front and half-back. Position the pattern pieces on the fabric, with the half-front and half-back of the skirt positioned along the fold, and cut out, allowing for a 1cm (½in) seam allowance and 2cm (¾in) for the hems. For the neckline, which is edged with grosgrain ribbon, cut close to the edge of the pattern.

2 Tack the pleat to each half-front of the bodice, then join the back and front of the bodice along the shoulder seams. Sew a hem either side of the back opening and sew some grosgrain ribbon around the neckline.

3 Overlap the bodice fronts and tack them together, then join them to the front of the skirt.

4 Tack the back of the bodice to the back of the skirt and join them. Sew a hem around the armholes then stitch the sides of the dress and hem around the bottom.

5 Sew a little white button at the top of the opening at the back and a button loop opposite using embroidery yarn. Tie a small, decorative bow with grosgrain ribbon and sew it on to the front of the dress.

SHOES

1 Enlarge the pattern for the sole and the upper of a shoe by 120% and cut the pieces out. Pin the pieces to the felt then cut the fabric out, leaving an 8mm (⅜in) seam allowance, except for around the opening, which is cut level with the edge.

2 Topstitch the opening, then close the upper of the shoe with a seam. Open out the seam, tack on the sole, lining up the centre of the sole with the centre of the upper, then machine stitch. Trim the felt to 3mm (⅛in) from the seam and turn out the shoe.

3 Cut the Liberty tape in half to make the straps. Sew one end of each strap on to one side of the shoe, on the inside.

4 Attach one part of a press stud to the other end of the strap and attach a little decorative button on top. Attach the other part of the press stud to the shoe, opposite.

5 Make the second shoe in the same way, the only difference being that the strap and the press stud are reversed.

HAIR TIES

1 Cut the lace in half and tie some flat, decorative half knots in it. Glue a knot carefully onto each hair tie.

OFF ON HOLIDAY

Materials

Cardboard suitcase
Spotty fabric
Checked fabric
Star print fabric
Elastic, 3mm (⅛in) wide

Small wooden stake
Iron-on wadding (batting)
White cotton for lining
Satin ribbon
White card, 2mm (¹⁄₁₆in) thick

1 Take the measurements of the lid, sides and bottom of the suitcase, and make a pattern joining up the three parts. Cut a piece from the iron-on wadding (batting), close to the edge of the pattern, and another from the spotty fabric, adding a 1cm (½in) seam allowance all around. Using an iron, attach the wadding to the back of the spotty fabric.

2 Cut two pockets from the checked fabric and the star print fabric, 6cm (2½in) wider than the suitcase and to the height of the sides.

3 Tack four pleats at the bottom of the pockets evenly spaced, 1cm (½in) apart along the length of the pockets, then turn the fabric under by 1cm (½in) all along the length and tack. Sew hems at the top and slip some elastic into them.

4 Cut a rectangle of wadding, 3cm (1¼in) high and of the same width as the suitcase. Glue it to the star print fabric using hot adhesive and trim, leaving a seam allowance. Fold the strip in half along the length, right sides together, stitch right along and turn out. Cut a small wooden stake, 2cm (¾in) smaller than the width of the suitcase and slip it into the strip.

5 Cut out a white lining using the spotty fabric inside as a pattern. Tack the bottom of the pockets and the rod onto the spotty fabric, then stitch. Stretch the elastic to adjust the pockets to the width of the suitcase, and attach them to either side using a few hand stitches. Tack the sides of the pockets. Sew a horizontal seam at the centre to divide the pockets in half.

6 Place the spotty fabric and its lining right sides together and stitch around, leaving a gap level with the bottom of the suitcase. Turn right side out and gently iron together.

7 Cut three pieces from the card in the dimensions of the lid, sides and bottom of the suitcase. Slip the card for the lid between the spotty fabric and its lining and put it in place, then sew a line of stitching level with the hinge to catch the two thicknesses of fabric together. Proceed in the same way for the sides, then for the bottom of the suitcase, and close the opening by hand.

8 Tie a bow from the satin ribbon and sew it at the top of the lid. Position the clothes holder inside the suitcase and attach it to the lid using a few stitches over the existing line of stitching in the suitcase.

CLOTHING DIRECTORY

Enlarge all the patterns by 140% (apart from the clothes for the Ballerina doll and Little Fairy doll, which are enlarged by 120%). The first figure refers to the instruction page, the second, in bold, to the pattern page. You can make a complete outfit like the ones shown here in this book or devise your own outfit by selecting from the different dresses, shoes, hats and matching accessories.

Accessories
Butterfly wings 107/**140**
Wand 107/**140**
Hair clips 38 & 10
Bouquet 54
Cherries 36
Cushion 75
Cupcakes 106/**140**
Tiara 90
Teddy 75/**130**
Tablecloth 107

Hats and caps
Bobble hat 98
Hat 68/132-133
Mop cap 46/**128**
Neckerchief 25
Veil 53/121

Shoes
Pumps 54 & 106/**119**
Boots 24 & 100/**118-119**
Ballet shoes 92/**119**
Shoes 30. 37, 45, 62. 84 & 108/**118**
Espadrilles 69/**118**
Mules 76/**119**

Skirts and trousers
Bloomers 45/**117**
Skirt 37/**125**
Pinafore dress 83/**125**
Underskirt 53, 90/**136**
Trousers 99/**139**
Dungarees 25/**120**

Underwear
Nightdress 74/**124**
Bloomers 15/**117**
Dressing gown 76/**134**
Vest 15/**116**

Dresses and pinafores
Dress 30/**122**. 44/**127**, 52/**129**, 60/**124**, 106/**140**. 108/**141**
Pinafore 31/**123**, 69/**131**
Tutu 90/**137**

Bags
Satchel 84
Bag 31/**121**
Barrel bag 92/**131** and 137

Top
Blouse 24/**124**, 36/**124**, 82/**135**
Sailor's top 99/**139**
Shrug 91
Leotard 91/**131**

Jackets and coats
Cape 38/**126**
Raincoat 98/**138**

115

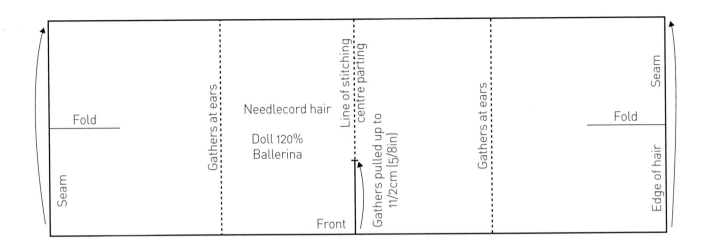

Fold

Seam

Gathers at ears

Needlecord hair

Doll 120%
Ballerina

Line of stitching
centre parting

Gathers pulled up to
11/2cm (5/8in)

Front

Gathers at ears

Fold

Seam

Edge of hair

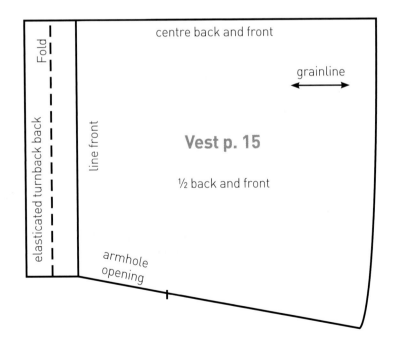

elasticated turnback back

Fold

line front

centre back and front

grainline

Vest p. 15

½ back and front

armhole
opening

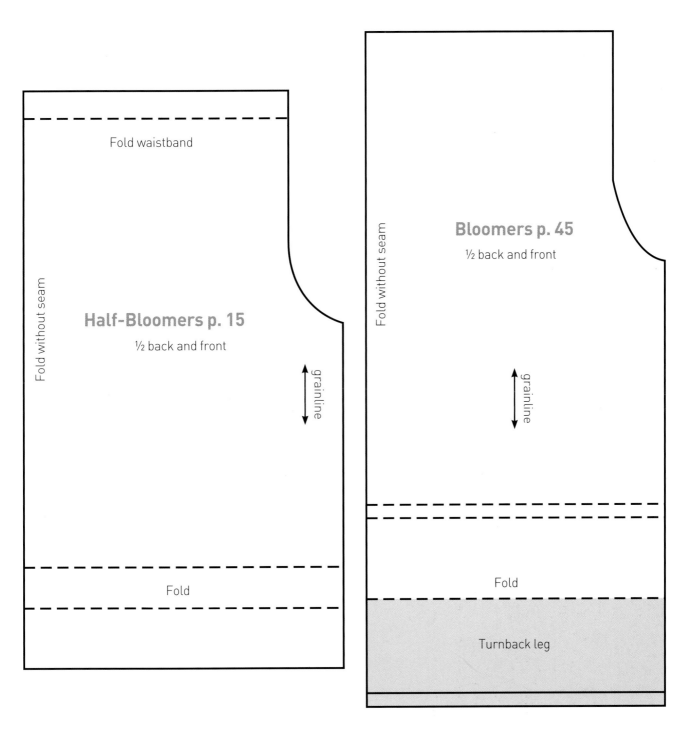

Fold waistband

Fold without seam

Half-Bloomers p. 15

½ back and front

grainline

Fold

Bloomers p. 45

½ back and front

Fold without seam

grainline

Fold

Turnback leg

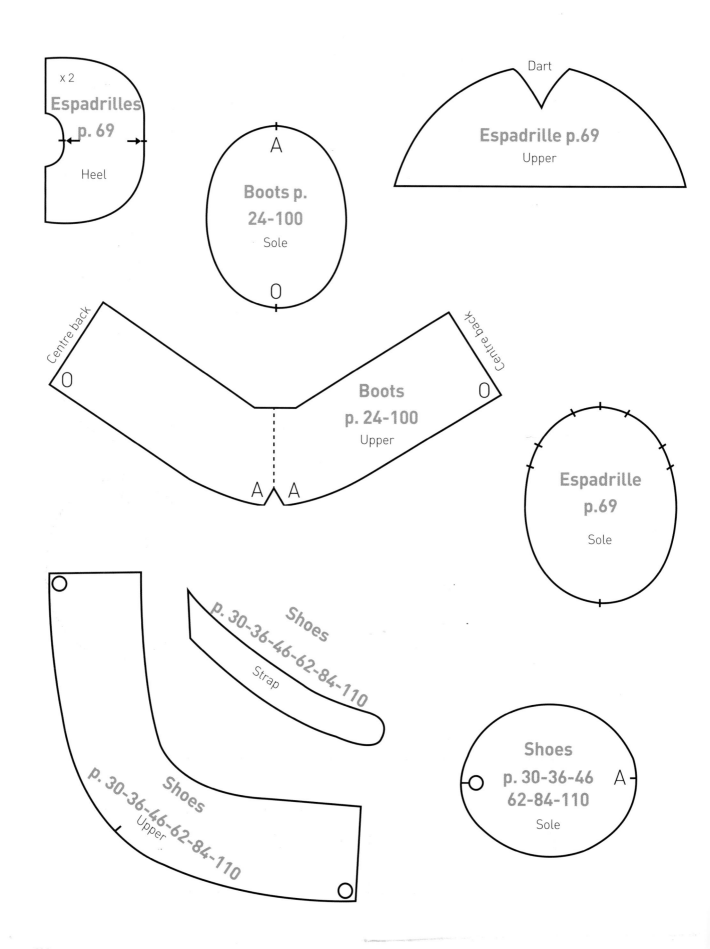

x 2

Espadrilles p. 69

Heel

A

Boots p. 24-100

Sole

O

Dart

Espadrille p.69

Upper

Centre back

O

Boots p. 24-100

Upper

O

Centre back

A A

Espadrille p.69

Sole

O

Shoes p. 30-36-46-62-84-110

Strap

Shoes p. 30-36-46-62-84-110

Upper

Shoes p. 30-36-46 62-84-110

Sole

A

O

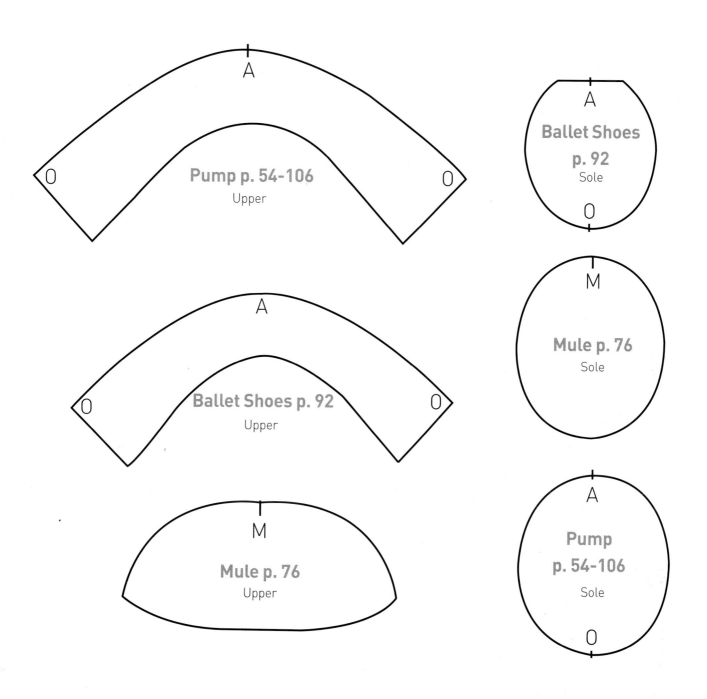

Pump p. 54-106
Upper

Ballet Shoes p. 92
p. 92
Sole

Ballet Shoes p. 92
Upper

Mule p. 76
Sole

Mule p. 76
Upper

Pump
p. 54-106
Sole

Turnback

Centre back

Centre back

Boots p. 24-100
Leg

Centre back

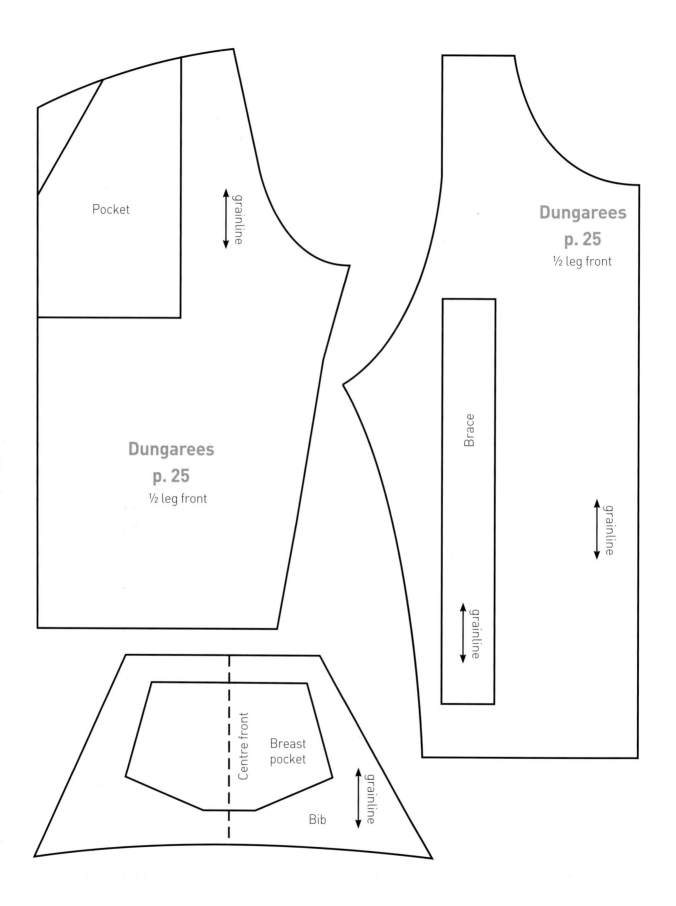

Pocket

grainline

Dungarees
p. 25
½ leg front

Dungarees
p. 25
½ leg front

Brace

grainline

grainline

Centre front

Breast
pocket

Bib

grainline

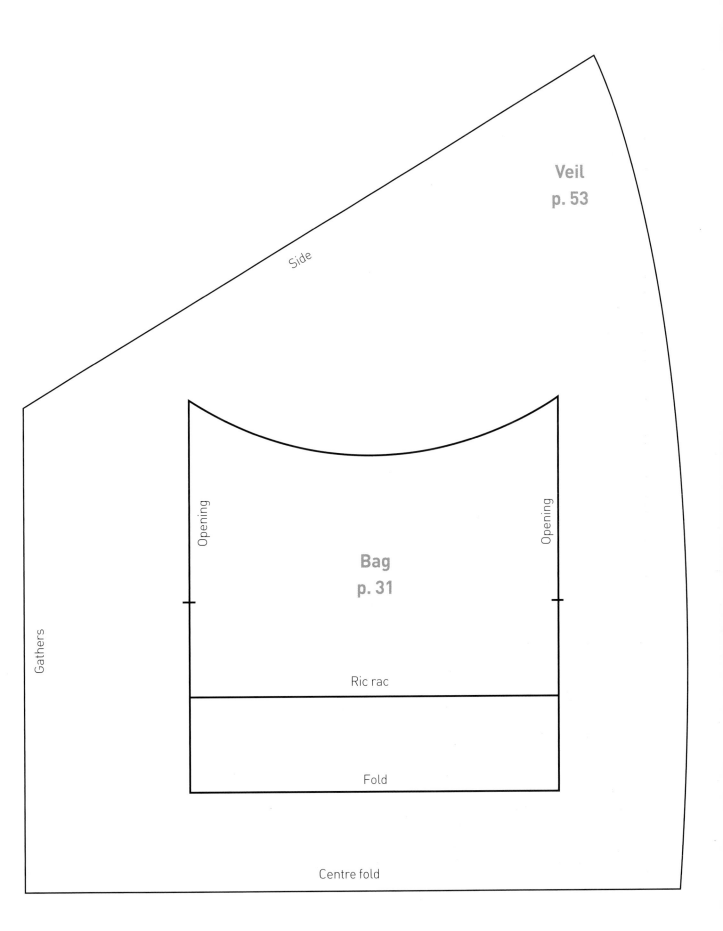

Veil
p. 53

Side

Opening

Opening

Gathers

Bag
p. 31

Ric rac

Fold

Centre fold

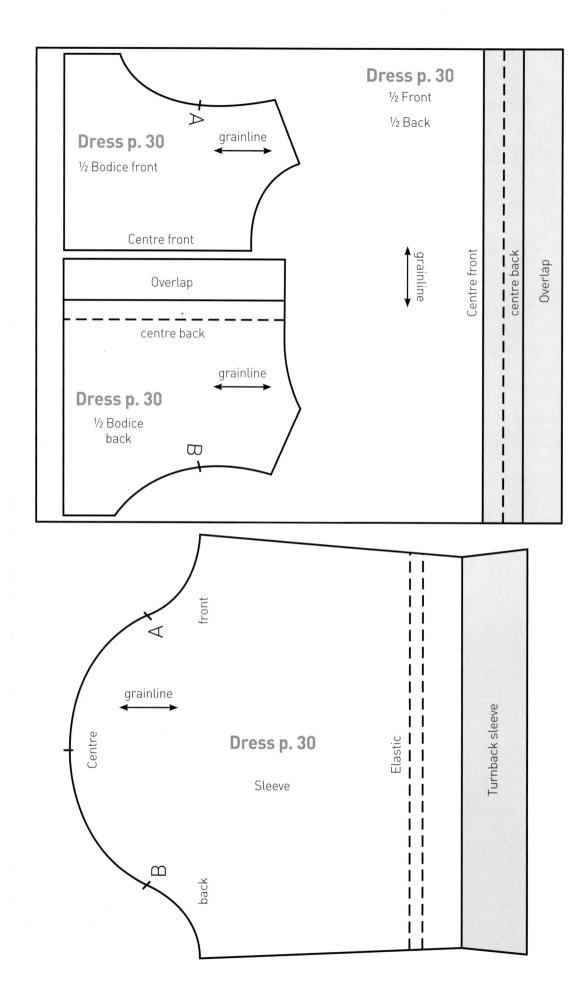

Dress p. 30

½ Bodice front

Centre front

A

grainline

Dress p. 30

½ Front

½ Back

grainline

Centre front

centre back

Overlap

Overlap

centre back

Dress p. 30

½ Bodice back

B

grainline

front

A

grainline

Centre

Dress p. 30

Sleeve

B

back

Elastic

Turnback sleeve

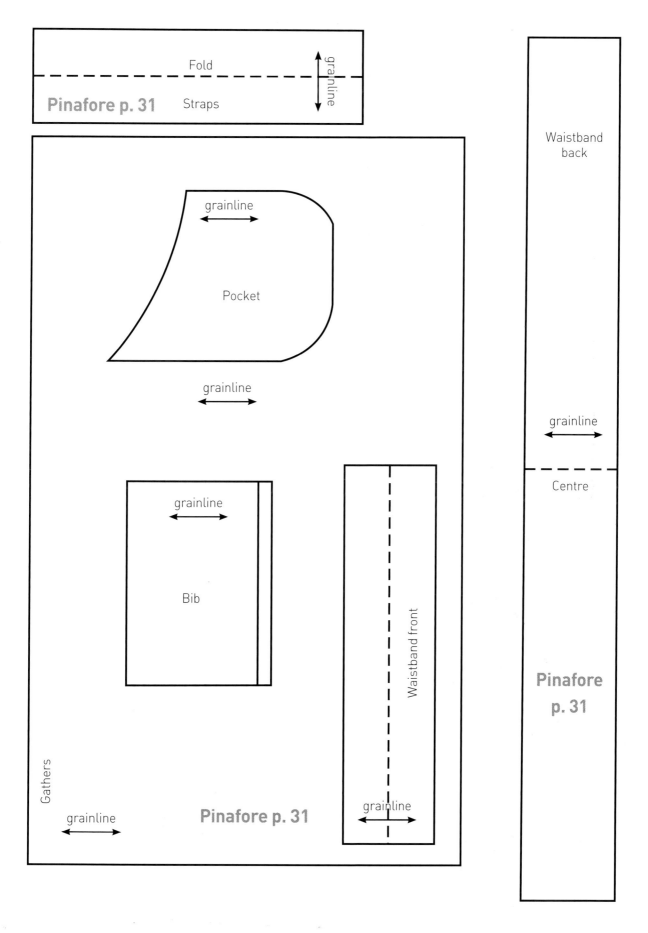

Fold

grainline

Pinafore p. 31   Straps

grainline

Pocket

grainline

grainline

Bib

Waistband front

grainline

Gathers

grainline

Pinafore p. 31

Waistband back

grainline

Centre

Pinafore p. 31

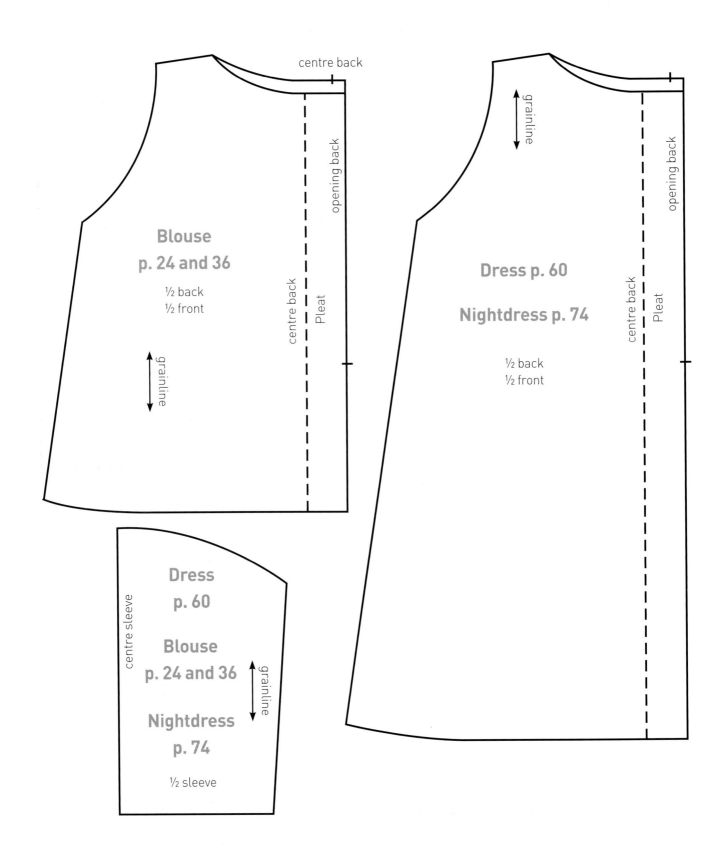

centre back

Blouse
p. 24 and 36

½ back
½ front

grainline

centre back

Pleat

opening back

grainline

Dress p. 60

Nightdress p. 74

½ back
½ front

centre back

Pleat

opening back

Dress
p. 60

Blouse
p. 24 and 36

Nightdress
p. 74

½ sleeve

centre sleeve

grainline

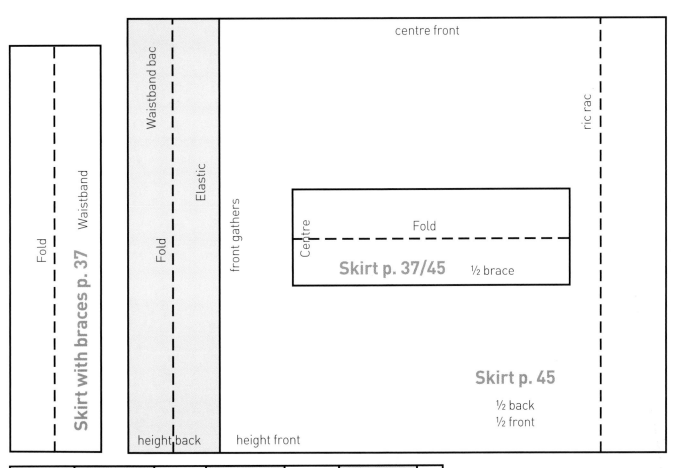

Skirt with braces p. 37

Fold

Waistband

Waistband bac

Elastic

Fold

height back

front gathers

height front

centre front

ric rac

Centre

Fold

Skirt p. 37/45

½ brace

Skirt p. 45

½ back
½ front

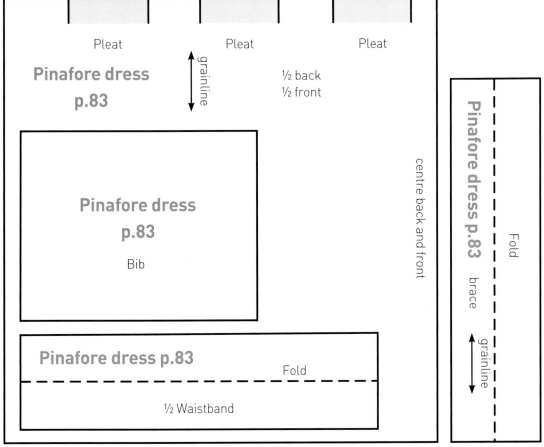

Pleat

Pleat

Pleat

Pinafore dress
p.83

grainline

½ back
½ front

Pinafore dress
p.83

Bib

centre back and front

Pinafore dress p.83

Fold

brace

grainline

Pinafore dress p.83

Fold

½ Waistband

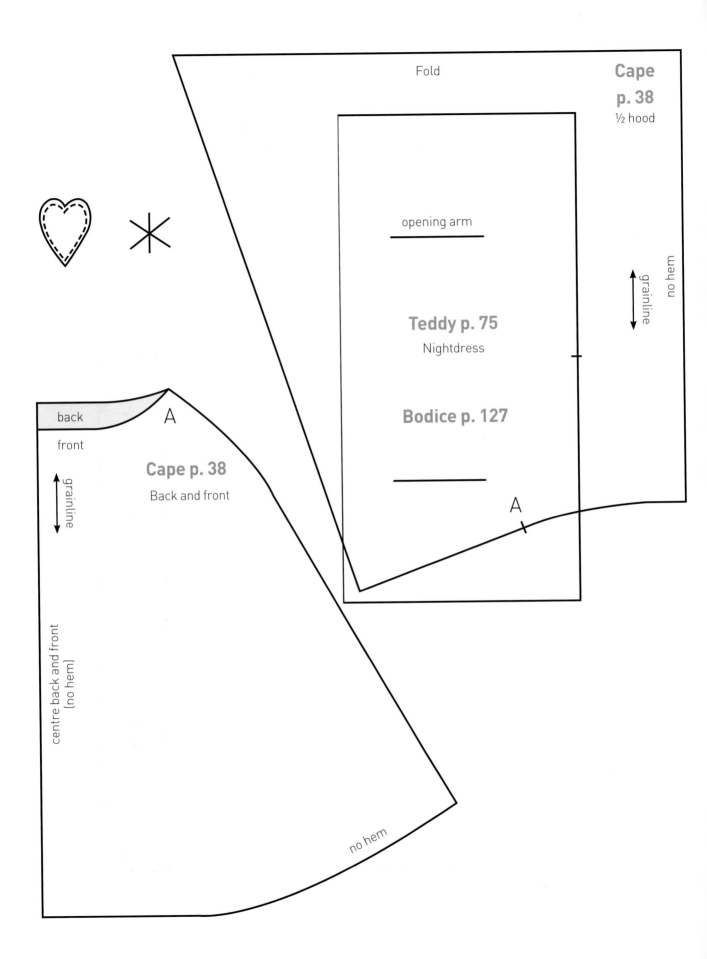

Fold

**Cape
p. 38**

½ hood

opening arm

no hem

grainline

Teddy p. 75

Nightdress

Bodice p. 127

A

A

back

front

grainline

Cape p. 38

Back and front

centre back and front
(no hem)

no hem

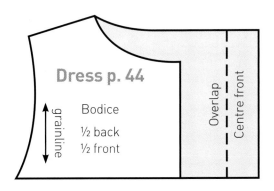

Dress p. 44

Bodice

½ back

½ front

grainline

Overlap

Centre front

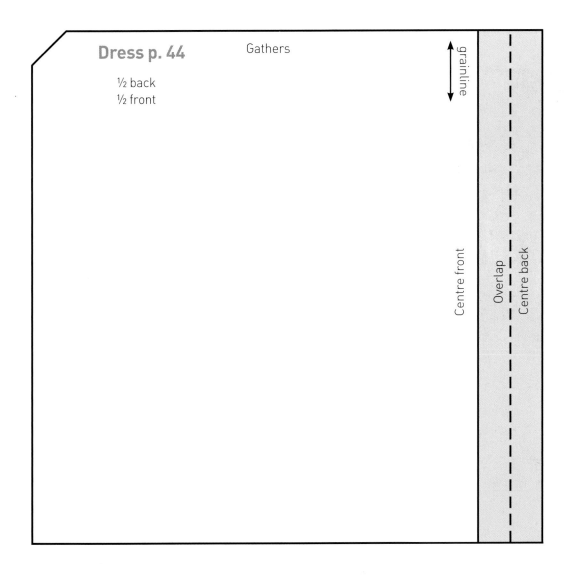

Dress p. 44

Gathers

½ back

½ front

grainline

Centre front

Overlap

Centre back

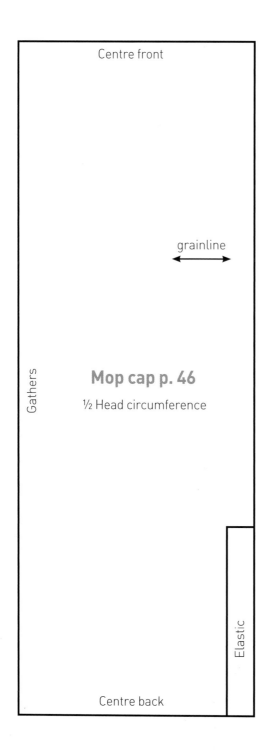

Centre front

grainline

Mop cap p. 46

½ Head circumference

Gathers

Elastic

Centre back

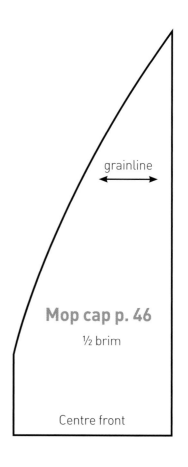

grainline

Mop cap p. 46

½ brim

Centre front

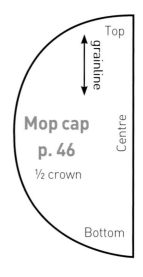

Top

grainline

Centre

Mop cap p. 46

½ crown

Bottom

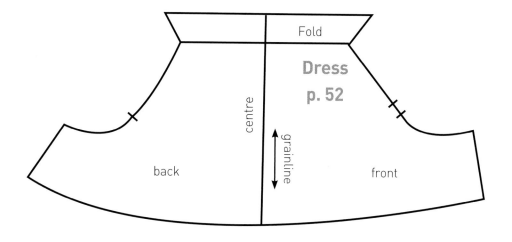

Fold

Dress p. 52

centre

grainline

back

front

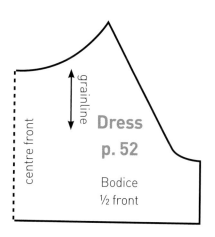

grainline

centre front

Dress p. 52

Bodice
½ front

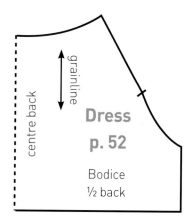

grainline

centre back

Dress p. 52

Bodice
½ back

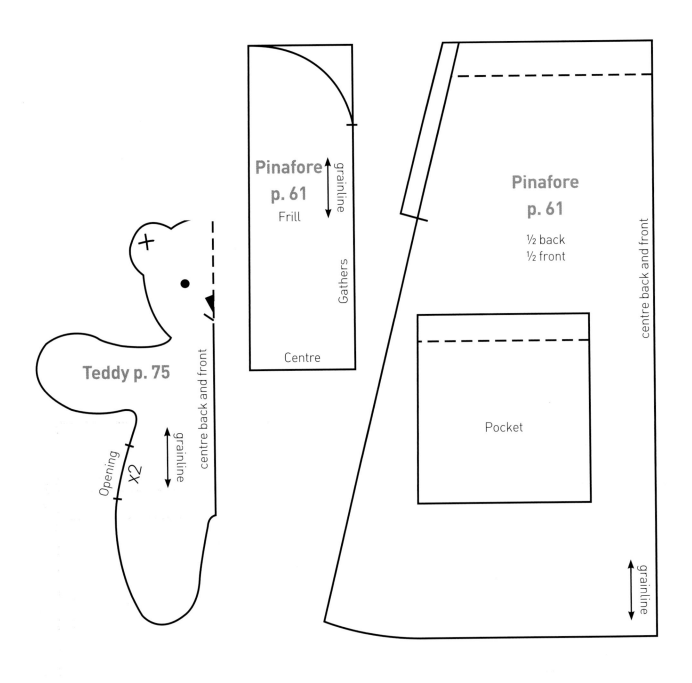

Pinafore p. 61 Frill

grainline

Gathers

Centre

Teddy p. 75

centre back and front

grainline

Opening

X2

Pinafore p. 61

½ back
½ front

centre back and front

Pocket

grainline

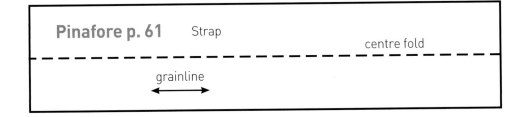

Pinafore p. 61 Strap

centre fold

grainline

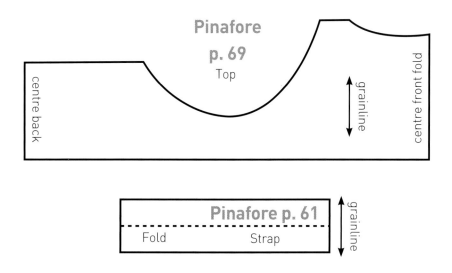

Pinafore
p. 69
Top

centre back

grainline

centre front fold

Pinafore p. 61

grainline

Fold   Strap

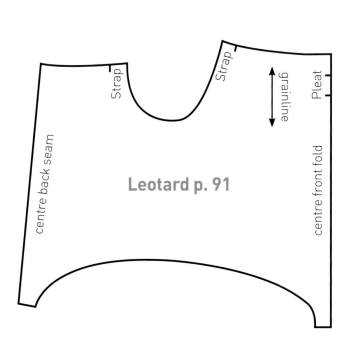

centre back seam

Strap

Strap

grainline

Pleat

centre front fold

Leotard p. 91

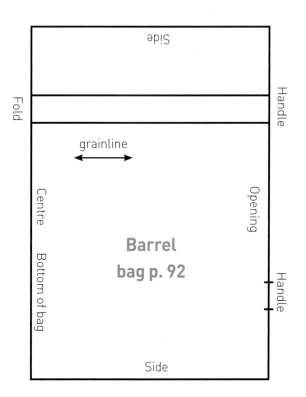

Side

Fold

Handle

grainline

Centre

Bottom of bag

Opening

Barrel
bag p. 92

Handle

Side

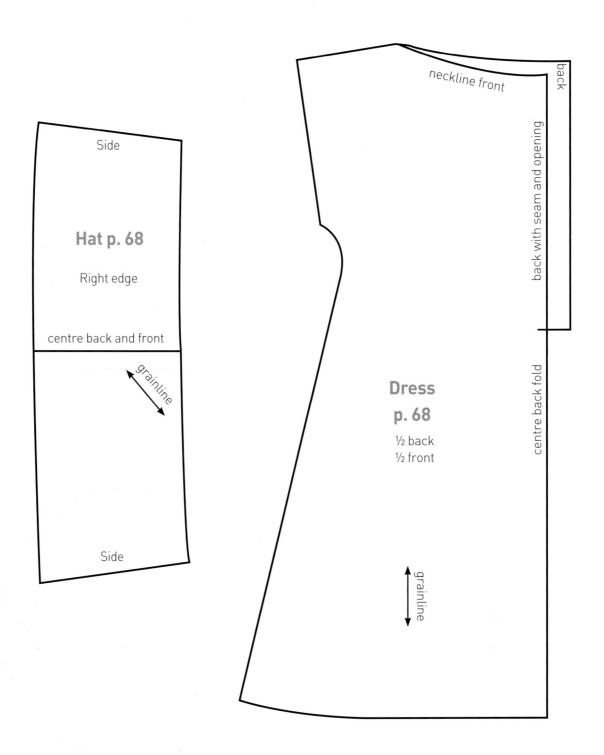

Side

Hat p. 68

Right edge

centre back and front

grainline

Side

neckline front

back

back with seam and opening

**Dress
p. 68**

½ back
½ front

centre back fold

grainline

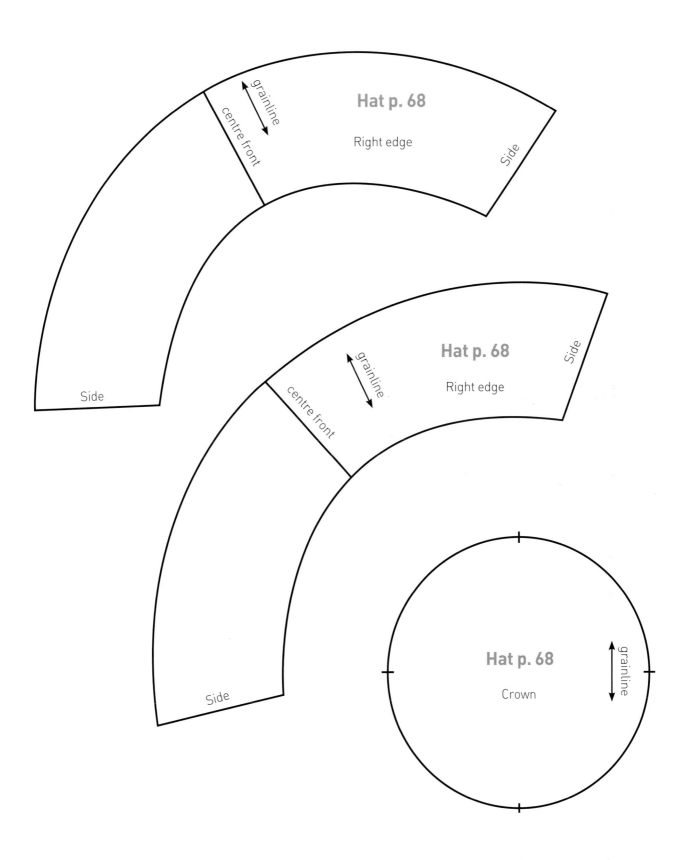

Hat p. 68
Right edge
Side
grainline
centre front
Side

Hat p. 68
Right edge
Side
grainline
centre front
Side

Hat p. 68
Crown
grainline

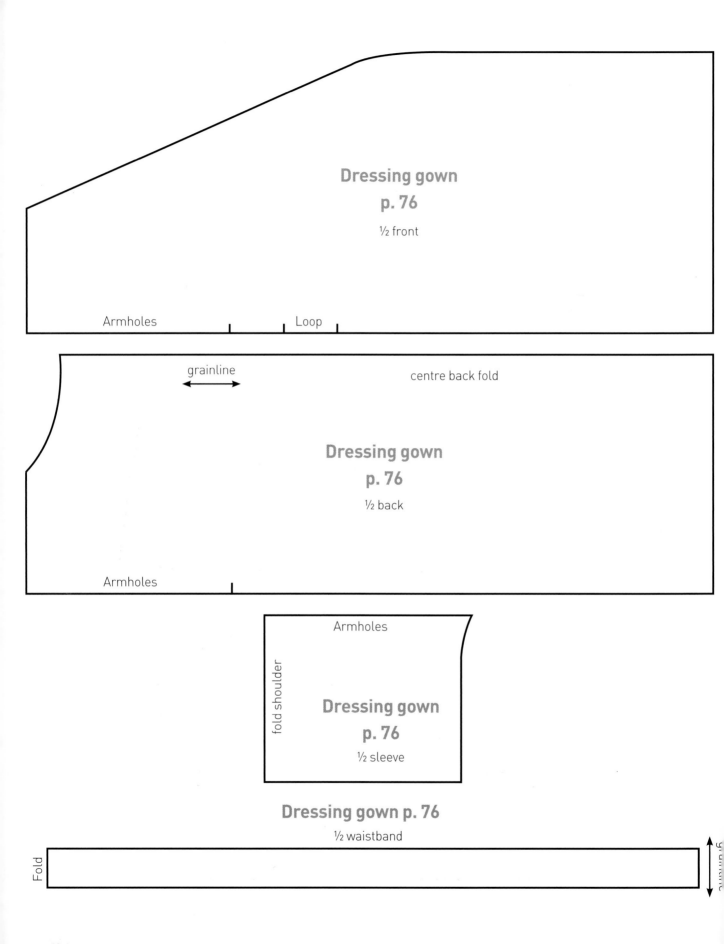

Dressing gown
p. 76

½ front

Armholes   Loop

grainline   centre back fold

Dressing gown
p. 76

½ back

Armholes

Armholes

fold shoulder

Dressing gown
p. 76

½ sleeve

Dressing gown p. 76

½ waistband

Fold   grainline

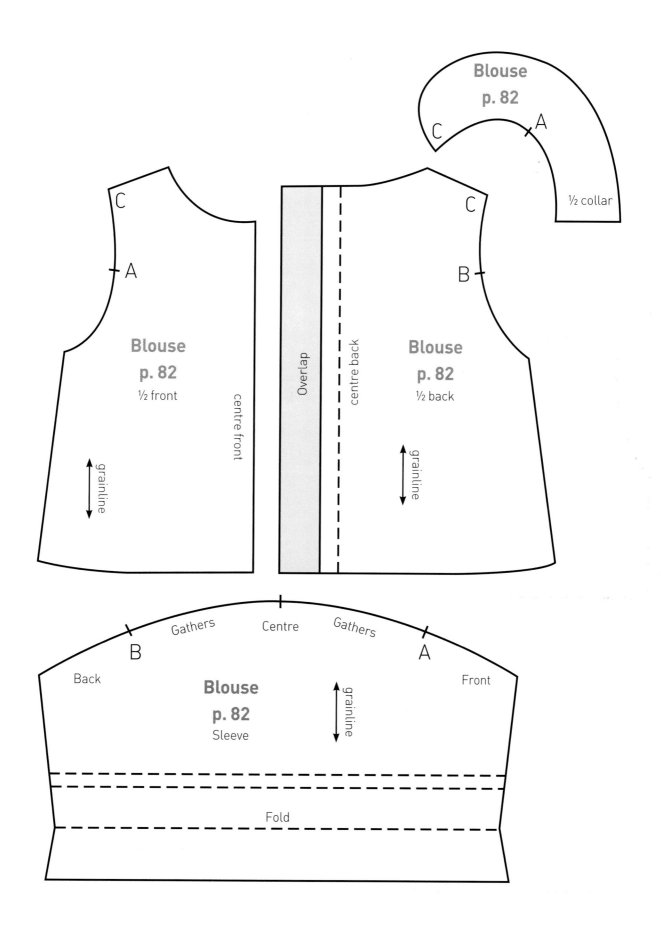

Blouse
p. 82

C

A

½ collar

C

A

Blouse
p. 82
½ front

centre front

grainline

Overlap

centre back

C

B

Blouse
p. 82
½ back

grainline

B

Gathers

Centre

Gathers

A

Back

Front

Blouse
p. 82
Sleeve

grainline

Fold

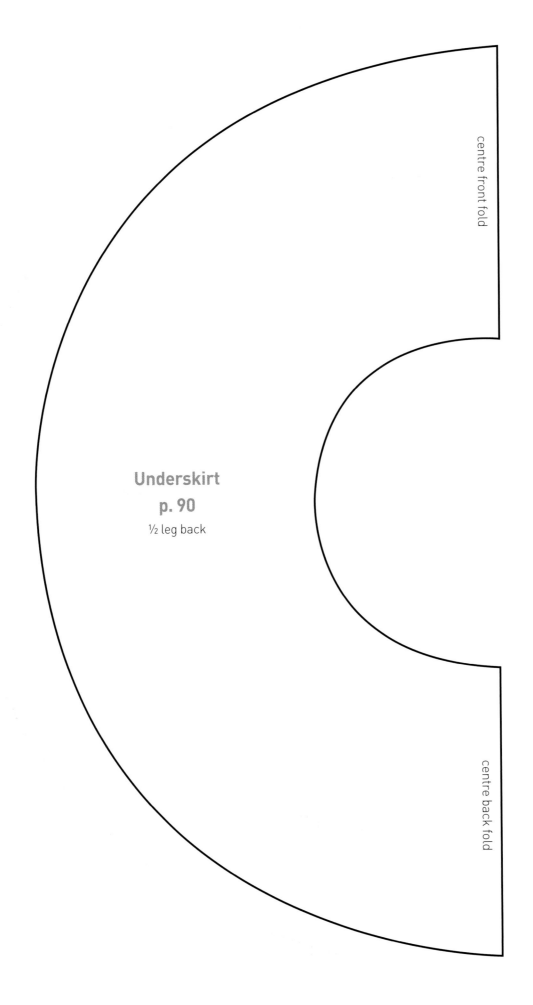

Underskirt
p. 90
½ leg back

centre front fold

centre back fold

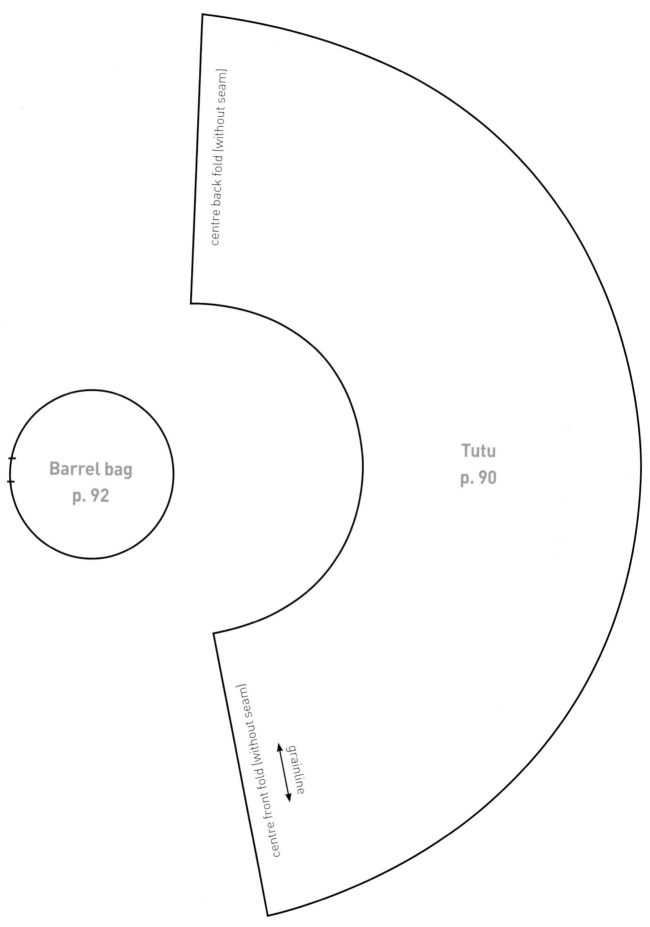

centre back fold (without seam)

Barrel bag
p. 92

Tutu
p. 90

centre front fold (without seam)

grainline

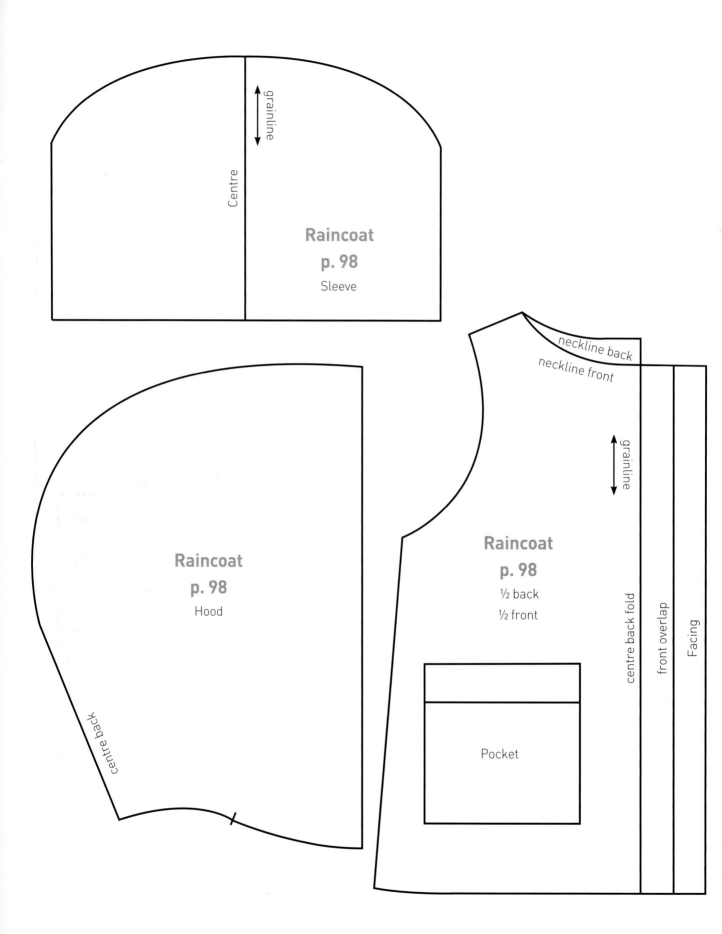

Raincoat

p. 98

Sleeve

Centre

grainline

Raincoat

p. 98

Hood

centre back

Raincoat

p. 98

½ back

½ front

neckline back

neckline front

grainline

centre back fold

front overlap

Facing

Pocket

138

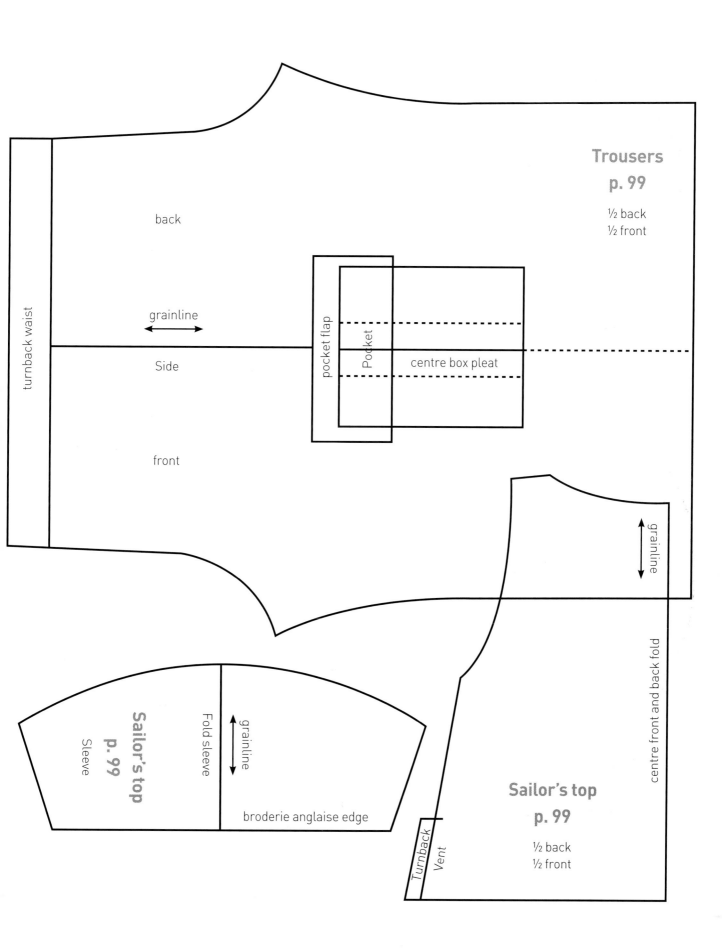

Trousers
p. 99

½ back
½ front

back

turnback waist

grainline

Side

front

pocket flap

Pocket

centre box pleat

grainline

centre front and back fold

Sailor's top
p. 99

½ back
½ front

Sailor's top
p. 99

Sleeve

Fold sleeve

grainline

broderie anglaise edge

Turnback

Vent

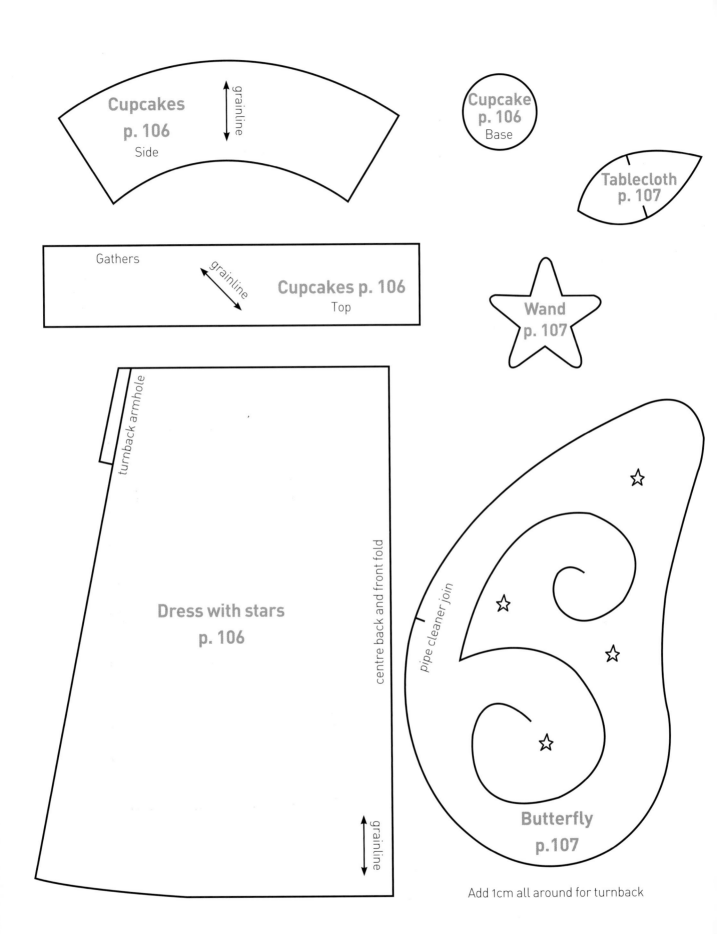

Cupcakes
p. 106
Side

grainline

Cupcake
p. 106
Base

Tablecloth
p. 107

Gathers

grainline

Cupcakes p. 106
Top

Wand
p. 107

turnback armhole

centre back and front fold

Dress with stars
p. 106

grainline

pipe cleaner join

Butterfly
p.107

Add 1cm all around for turnback

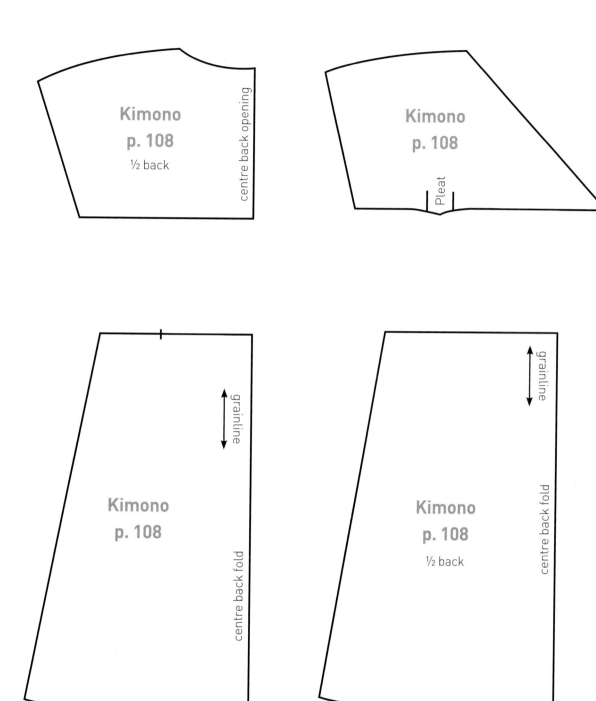

Kimono
p. 108
½ back

centre back opening

Kimono
p. 108

Pleat

grainline

Kimono
p. 108

centre back fold

grainline

Kimono
p. 108
½ back

centre back fold

INDEX

SUPPLIERS

La droguerie
Ribbons, lace and other accessories
www.ladroguerie.com

Bouts de tissus
Fabrics
www.boutsdetissusrueil.fr

Entrée des fournisseurs
Ribbons, lace and other accessories
www.entreedesfournisseurs.fr

Mokuba
Ribbons, braids and lace
www.mokuba.fr

France Duval-Stalla
Fabrics
www.franceduvalstalla.com

Marie et Gustave
Fabrics
www.marieetgustave.com

Ki-sign création
Hotfix rhinestones and velvet
www.ki-sign.com

To Pierre, my brother,
my hero who left us too soon...
and to Elie, Noé, Cécile and little Lily.

ACKNOWLEDGEMENTS

Thank you to Lisa, John, Nicolas, my parents, my sister Véro and all my large family.

Thank you to France Duval-Stalla, Corinne from la Droguerie, Chantal from Marie et Gustave, Lisa from L'entrée des fournisseurs, Edith from Ki-Sign, Dominique from Bouts de Tissus, Nathalie at Indémodable and Mokuba for their generosity, confidence in and enthusiasm for my dolls!

Thank you to Sandrine, Magali, Anne, my faithful friends Christine and Katia, as well as my pupils for their help and encouragement.

Thank you to Pascale, Dominique, Frédéric, Sonia and Vania, not forgetting Nina too, a fantastic team, who have presented this sweet children's fantasy world so beautifully.

Published by Hachette Livre (43, quai de Grenelle, Paris Cedex 15)
© Hachette Livre (Marabout) 2013
Printed in China by RR Donnelley
Copyright: September 2013
ISBN: 978-1-4463-0484-6
1-4463-0484-1

Layout: Frédéric Voisin
Text and adaptation: Dominique Montembault